Attachment Narrative Therapy

Attachment Narrative Therapy

Integrating Systemic, Narrative and Attachment Approaches

Rudi Dallos

Open University Press

Open University Press
McGraw-Hill Education
McGraw-Hill House
Shoppenhangers Road
Maidenhead
Berkshire
England
SL6 2QL

email: enquiries@openup.co.uk
world wide web : www.openup.co.uk

and Two Penn Plaza, New York, NY 10121-2289, USA

First Published 2006
Reprinted 2007

A catalogue record of this book is available from the British Library

ISBN 10: 0335 21417 7 (pb)   0335 21418 5 (hb)
ISBN 13: 9780335214174 (pb)   9780335214181 (hb)

Library of Congress Cataloging-in-Publication Data
CIP data applied for

Typeset by YHT Ltd
Printed in UK by Bell & Bain Ltd., Glasgow

Contents

Foreword

"Emotion is a leading element in the system that organises interaction between intimates"

(Sue Johnson, 1988)

This book develops a theoretical base for exploring how we can work therapeutically 'within' and 'between': how people construct their relational context, and how the relational context influences people. This is a major theoretical achievement, bringing together the domains of attachment theory, systemic practice and narrative approaches to therapy. Both attachment and systems theories are large bodies of well researched clinical theories, and with the more recent narrative approaches, provide a means of theorising emotion in relational terms, in ways that help people create narratives of how they healed their relationships.

Attachment theory focuses our attention on emotional regulation and helps us trust emotion as a cue to our clients' needs. Family and intimate relationships can either foster or erode the sense of security of its members, which can be influential in the development of distress or resilience. The implications for practice of integrating attachment theory into systemic therapy are far reaching: helping people name and regulate their emotions; learning to stand in the emotional shoes of the other, and tolerating the negative emotional states of intimates; paying more attention to patterns of comforting and self-soothing; and processing emotional experience. It is probably too easy to get lost in content and pragmatic issues, particularly if we choose to avoid the intensity and power of emotional experience in our work. Attachment Narrative Therapy is not catharsis, rather it provides a framework for thinking – processing emotional experience, expanding our range of emotional responding in relation to intimate others, and integrating our emotional experience.

The systemic approach to narrative espoused in Attachment Narrative Therapy has a number of aspects. ANT explores the connections between the beliefs and stories about relationships and events from the perspectives of everyone involved in the network of concern. It provides a framework to generate multiple perspectives about these relationships and events, whilst exploring the fit between older and more current stories or accounts about self, others, events and the connections between them. Thus with the integration of attachment thinking, ANT offers a clear framework for addressing the developmental, emotional and social implications of preferred ideas and action generated in therapeutic work.

In this elegant and well articulated synthesis, Rudi Dallos offers an integrative framework for practice that offers practitioners and their clients more choice. Therapists act as process consultants, in ways that are culturally attuned. They both follow and lead, slowing down the experience, reflecting on process, and helping to develop new interactional patterns, for example, around soothing and comfort, along with a shared account of how change happened. ANT prioritises the need to create a secure emotional connection as the context for problem solving, based on the assumption that people already have problem solving skills and that relational issues loaded with attachment significance are the ones people struggle to resolve. We cannot readily experience our skills when we are afraid or threatened by loss. Attachment theory speaks to our vulnerability and validates it. In our ANT workshops, offered up and down the UK, we find practitioners are seeking a map for relationships and for change, that captures how we construct our inner worlds and regulate our emotional arousal, and how that influences how we interact with our emotional intimates, in reciprocal fashion. This book is timely. It captures our interest in how emotion communicates to the self and to others.

"Love, work and knowledge are the wellsprings of our lives, they should also govern it"
(Wilhelm Reich,)

Arlene Vetere, 2006

Acknowledgement

This book is about attachments and I want to thank all the people in my life – friends, partners, children and colleagues – who have supported me in producing this work. It is partly about relationships like ours and is also a product of the support, both emotional and intellectual, that they have shown.

I want to thank Jon Reed, Shonna Mullen, Cathy Thompson and Jacinta Evans for their support with this and many other projects with OU Press/ McGraw Hill. They offer excellent examples of good attachment to and with their writers support, encouragement, empathy and clear guidance.

A massive thank you to Arlene Vetere for her invaluable support and for the privilege of working with her up and down the country running our workshops on ANT. I also want to thank Pat Crittenden for her inspirational teaching and support.

Finally to my children, Jasmine, Alex and Tim, who inspired this book, I thank you for returning in heaps the, at times limited, attachment support I have been able to give you.

Introduction

This book is about what many therapists of various theoretical persuasions do in their work with people and their families, which is to draw on a variety of ideas, theories and techniques. We can describe this as eclecticism or a pragmatic approach. However, our choices regarding what we decide to draw on are shaped by our experience and understanding about what may be missing and what is available to us. I am writing this book from the perspective of someone with a strong commitment to systemic family therapy. Along with many other therapists employing systemic ideas I have also developed a strong interest in approaches drawn from social constructionism. The narrative therapies add the important dimension of an emphasis on meaning and language as the vehicle whereby patterns and problems are constructed in families. Importantly, they also describe the process of therapy as a co-constructive process.

However, I have had some nagging questions about the role of emotions and attachments in families' lives and in the process of my work with families. Some of these thoughts and doubts came to a head for me during a period when I was working exclusively with families presenting with problems of eating disorders. In session after session, and with family after family, I was experiencing the therapy sessions as a tense, reluctant, emotionally draining process. I kept feeling that I was having to 'make' some conversation happen in the room and that encouraging people to talk was hard work. I started to wonder what this was about: was I losing what therapeutic skills I had? Were the families attending very resentful about the referral process, perhaps? Or, was it to do with their views of therapy and perhaps how they saw talking, especially about relationships? The last question raises some important issues for postmodern approaches to therapy which eschew the idea of family patterns or types. A starting point for early family therapy (Hoffman 1981; Dallos and Draper 2005) had been a search for the Holy Grail of linking family patterns with various forms of disturbance. For example, the idea of a double-binding pattern in families as being linked to the emergence of 'psychotic' symptoms.

A colleague introduced me to some recent developments in attachment theory, an approach I had put aside years earlier because I regarded it as engaging in simple typologies and potentially mother-blaming practices. However, the recent developments included interesting ideas about the links between narratives and attachment experiences (Main et al. 1985; Crittenden

1997). In fact these developments seemed to cover just the ground that had first interested me in family therapy. They were drawing out links between patterns of family relationships and how these shape different forms of internal worlds, including the narratives we develop about ourselves and others, and in particular the narratives about feelings, relationships and attachments. Something also very important about this work was that it was not pathologizing families. The family patterns were not intended to suggest pejorative claims about how they were manufacturing forms of pathology but instead how these were shaping forms of internal experience that fitted with the family dynamics. I became increasingly excited about drawing together these strands: family systemic patterns, attachment and narratives. I hope this book serves to share some of this excitement and helps a little to encourage others to develop and take these ideas further.

Let me start by offering a small extract from my final conversation with one of the families that I worked with during this period and from whom I learnt so much. The interview is in our final session with Barbara's family. Barbara had been suffering with anorexia. She was living alternative days with each of her separated parents (Harry and Tania). Her weight had stabilized and she was back at school and doing well:

RD:	What were your expectations of what this [therapy] would be like?
Tania:	I think we all thought it would be pretty stilted, difficult to talk and horrible long silences with everyone staring at their feet, waiting for someone else to say something and a wish not to expose any personal things...
Harry:	Being analysed I think...
Tania:	That's right, yes, wanting to curl up and hide everything. That was what my view of what this would be like.
Harry:	Mine was we don't need this but we've got to do it because we have been asked ... I must admit I have softened on that a bit since but that was my first impression ... let's sweat it out.
RD:	What about you Barbara?
Barbara:	I thought it was a really bad idea, it would be awful and I wouldn't say anything at all. Being put on the spot and made to say things you didn't really want to. I just thought it would be really awful.
RD:	I'm not fishing for compliments but how has it been different to what you expected?
Tania:	For a start I thought it was much easier to talk, much more relaxed ... I was surprised and impressed about how easy it

> was and how everyone was able, how we all talked. We are
> not, and particularly Harry, doesn't like talking ... I've been
> really pleased how my family, we have all talked together.
> Talked here much more easily than we would have at home,
> with you adjudicating, and perhaps triggered off questions
> that would have been difficult to get around to in the
> claustrophobic atmosphere at home, and we'd get wound up
> about it.

I worked with Barbara and her family for about a year as we explored their
struggles with the anorexia that had come into their lives. Anorexia is a
tortuous, slow, painful and desperate condition which attaches itself to bright
young people and sucks the life out of them. I liked Barbara and her parents
and I think they came to quite like and trust me, and the fact that we were
able to develop a positive relationship I think led to my work with them being
helpful.

Some of the key ingredients of this book are in this brief extract. The
family viewed the prospect of therapy with considerable trepidation. In particular they appear to regard talking as difficult: 'We are not, and particularly
Harry, doesn't like talking'. On the other hand they go on to say that as they
discovered that it could be quite relaxed with me this fear and their ability to
talk changed. This also eloquently expresses what family therapy is about:
being with an adjudicator, which offers a different context that enables
talking about difficult things to take place.

Family therapy has accompanied the shifts in the social 'sciences', such as
psychology, counselling and sociology, to an emphasis on the centrality of
meaning and meaning-making. This has come within the broad umbrella of
social constructionism which has proposed that language and talking are the
central aspects of human life. This has meant a shift away from a focus on
behaviour and patterns of interactions to processes of meaning-making.
Inherent in this has also been the recognition that this framework requires a
shift in the position of therapists and researchers from being 'objective
observers' to being 'active participants'. Interestingly, in the account above
we can see nice examples of these points. The family members state what
their expectations and beliefs were on attending family therapy. The situation
itself held a meaning for them. A core part of this was that they seemed to
view the prospect of therapy with trepidation. Importantly, they also seem to
be saying that they were aware that a central part of the experience was that
they became, and realized that they needed to be, actively involved in their
own meaning-making processes. In fact they describe using me as an adjudicator in the work that they needed to do with each other.

Their eloquent account also highlights the issue which is of central importance in this book: the issue of feelings. The meanings the people in this family held about therapy were suffused with feelings: 'A wish not to expose any personal things', 'horrible long silences', wanting to 'curl up and hide', 'being put on the spot', 'it would be really awful'. These quotes and my own experience with the family indicated that they felt anxious and frightened. Moreover they had a belief that talk was perhaps dangerous, that it could make things worse not better: 'the claustrophobic atmosphere at home, and we'd get *wound up* about it'. Sometimes it seems to me that social constructionist accounts of meaning-making lack this vitally important component. Talking is suffused with emotions. When we talk, and even when we think about talking emotions are activated. Meaning-making is a passionate not a dispassionate affair. Maybe we have been over-influenced by discourses, arguably Western, patriarchal ones, which promote a view of people and social interaction as dispassionate and rational (Foucault 1975; Bruner 1990; Gergen 1999). Interestingly, developmental research suggests that emotions are central from the earliest age and that we often forget the importance of positive feelings and how they shape relationships (Trevarthen 1992). A vivid reminder here is the extreme distress that mothers feel with infants (variously labelled as Aspergers spectrum or autistic disorder) who have difficulty in displaying and reciprocating feelings.

Personal Connections

Are there other reasons why am I interested in attachment theory? An important part of my answer to this is that it helps make some sense of my own life in a more convincing way than do other perspectives or theories. One strand of this for me is that as a refugee I had experienced some painful separations when we fled from Hungary in the 1956 'uprising'. I became separated from my maternal grandmother, '*nagymama*', who I loved dearly and who loved me, and from my younger sister, Ildi; and once in England I also experienced several very painful separations from my mother. So perhaps I have an unusual background and this explains my eventual interest. Maybe these early experiences created a need to explore these feelings which I had attempted to shut off from awareness. Attachment theory suggests that whether our early experiences involve extraordinary, or more ordinary, events, nevertheless they have a dramatic impact on our lives. Everyday separations, such as a first day at nursery, can for a young child be experienced as powerfully as can more apparently significant ones.

Orientation of the book: systemic family therapy, attachment theory and narrative therapy

This book is written from the perspective of a systemic therapist looking outwards to make connections with attachment and narrative perspectives. The orientation of the book would be very different if it were written by an attachment theorist or a narrative therapist looking outwards to make connections between the two approaches. One of the aims of the book is to consider the links between meaning-making processes in families and attachment patterns. More broadly this is part of a wider aim to consider how the social world of the family shapes and is in turn shaped by the internal worlds of the family members. But this already runs the risk of constructing a division which we then need to reconcile. Arguably the internal and the social worlds are not distinct or separable aspects, rather they are inextricably interwoven. This has been termed intersubjectivity: the idea that personal experience is embedded in a sense of being with or being a part of another's experience. This idea of the self as part of a system of social processes is central to social constructionism and to systemic theory.

Attachment theory in its careful observation of early interactional processes and the impact these have on developing internal states adds detail to the picture of this meaning-making process. One of the guiding themes of this book will to be to explore what attachment theory has to offer to an understanding of meaning-making in families. Specifically, it looks at how such meaning-making takes shape as the child develops the accounts and narratives that he or she comes to hold about his or her experiences, which at the same time shape the child's identity. Alongside this, attachment theory can add to our understanding of how children learn to communicate and the patterns of communications in families.

Why attachment narrative therapy (ANT): why we need the integration of attachment theory, systemic perspectives and narrative therapy

Some of the reasons for the need for this integration can be suggested by first outlining what I see as some limitations of each perspective. I do not want this to be a catalogue of complaints about each of the perspectives but an overview of some of my thoughts and experiences on employing ideas and methods from each of them.

Systemic theory and therapy
- Neglecting individual experience
- Lack of a developmental perspective
- Recent family therapy neglects patterns
- Neglect of links between family patterns and problems

Systemic therapy (Dallos and Draper 2005) now embraces a wide spectrum of ideas. It offers a radical position in its move to an interpersonal, relational view of problems away from the essentially intrapsychic orientations of preceding models. Rather than viewing problems as resulting from various forms of individual deficit or pathology it offers a view of problems as resulting from relationship processes and patterns. This had profound implications for treatment and in terms of the ethics of therapy. It helped us to move away from positions of blaming and imposing treatments on people whose distress was a response to family dynamics rather than something inside them. However, this revolution of thinking may have moved us to place such a great emphasis on pattern that we started to overlook the nature of individual experience in families and how different identities and personalities develop. The person became lost in the complexity of discussion about processes and patterns. Interestingly, systemic family therapy has more recently moved away even from a consideration of patterns to an emphasis on meaning-making processes. Drawing on social constructionist perspectives there has been a shift towards an emphasis on the family as being one of the significant locations where meanings are constructed in the flux of daily family life. Therapy, rather than attempting to find patterns, became more of a pragmatic process of encouraging change without specifying what direction this might or should take.

This shift can be linked with a pragmatic orientation that traces its origins back to strategic and pragmatic orientations advocated by early pioneers such as Haley (1963, 1987), Watzlawick et al. (1974) and Palazzzoli et al. (1978). The criterion of successful therapy is 'what works is what works'. Haley (1963, 1987) had argued that the search for patterns, causal understanding of development of problems, exploration of family patterns and how these link to problems could be seen as questions and priorities for researchers. However, they could become irrelevant distractions for therapists since, for example, trying to understand how problems can come about is not only futile given the complexity of family life, but also it may not assist us very much in finding ways we can help families to change.

Though some of these arguments are compelling they can ultimately leave us in a purely pragmatic stance and without a way of building theory to guide and develop our practice. Instead, I want to argue that it is important and useful to consider the experiences of family members and how particular patterns can be seen to shape their developments. This does not need to imply a return to taking an expert position but rather to taking a tentative, propositional stance from which we can think about patterns and developing identities from an 'as if' position. This may be guided by helpful hypotheses we hold about families.

As with systemic theory some nagging questions arise regarding narrative therapy:

Narrative theory and therapy
- How do narratives develop?
- Do people have differences in their narrative abilities/'skills'
- What are the links between narratives and life events and family patterns?

Many systemic family therapists have added or even moved over to a narrative approach to their work with families. As we will see in Chapter 3 this draws on social constructionist perspectives which emphasize meaning-making as being central to human activity and specifically the idea that the key way people do this is through the construction of narratives or stories about their lives. Particular narratives, such as a story of a family member as suffering with a 'mental illness', holds massive implications for how the person regards themself, how others see them, how they are treated, what actions are imposed on them and what hopes and fears are jointly held about their future life, or sometimes more accurately their lack of a future! Narrative work with families can be elegant in the way different, new, less oppressive and abusive stories can be co-constructed with families.

However, some nagging questions have presented themselves to me in this kind of work. To start with it may be that families and family members differ in how able they are to engage in this way of working. There is an emerging body of research that suggests that placing our experiences into narratives is a sophisticated skill which develops gradually through childhood and needs to be fostered and nurtured. Also, the content of narratives will be shaped by real, lived experiences. In families where there have been extensive experiences of deprivation and abusive relationships it is likely that they develop narratives that correspond with these experiences. So they come to see themselves in pessimistic and self-deprecating ways. However, importantly for narrative therapies, it may be that not only is the content of their narrative important but also how it is organized. Research on narrative development suggests that the organization of narratives is related to family processes and to mental health. Importantly, recent developments in attachment theory suggest that emotional processes in families shape narrative processes, such as the extent to which narratives are distortions of events, to what extent they are coherent, include accounts of other people's feelings and thoughts and are able to integrate events. It may be helpful, for example, for narrative therapy to consider what families are able to comprehend and utilize from therapeutic conversations and reflecting teams. Without taking this into account we may be overlooking the possibility that sometimes we are talking to ourselves and not them. An understanding of how they have learnt to place their experiences into narratives and the ways that they transform events, for example a pattern of excluding the contribution of feelings, attachments and relationships to their problems, may help our ability to talk and construct new narratives with families.

Attachment Theory
- Overly biological – deterministic?
- Mother-blaming?
- Is a dyadic focus too simple?

As we will explore in Chapters 1, 2 and 3, attachment theory offers a relational account of how identities develop in families and the more recent version of attachment theory also offers an account of how our narratives develop. However, attachment theory can be seen as overly narrow in its emphasis on the dyadic process. Worse, this has predominantly been a focus on mother–child patterns with some implications of mother-blaming for the development of insecurity in their infants. Arguably attachment theory has also adopted an overly biological view of the basis of attachments rather than considering the socio-cultural processes that shape what is regarded as appropriate, good parenting, appropriate levels of bonding and the role of mothers and fathers.

Do we need ANT – a new therapeutic approach?

John Byng-Hall (1995) argued persuasively that systems theory can benefit from the inclusion of ideas from attachment theory and that in fact there is considerable overlap between the approaches. Bowlby (1969, 1973) in developing attachment theory drew on systemic ideas in that he viewed attachment as an interactional system between the child and caregiver. However, Byng-Hall (1995) also argued that there is no need to develop yet another form of therapy. I partly agree with his view and this book, like his pioneering and fascinating work, is an attempt to bring into family therapy some useful perspective from attachment and narrative therapies. However, I think it may be helpful to designate this as an approach because there are aspects of the three approaches that do make up a greater whole. Also, it helps us to think about issues involved in integrating these perspectives rather than remaining at the level of an eclectic mix. There is the question of the level of integration that is possible. I am not claiming to have produced a revision of all three theories. The guiding framework of the book is a systemic one, which arguably is a meta-theory, with its broad emphasis on the relational nature of experience, patterns and difference, that can embrace a variety of other models.

The aim of this book then is to draw attention to some important points of difference as well as the connections between these perspectives and to a synthesis of an approach to working with people and their families which is to some extent distinct. Attachment theory, like systemic therapy, has been in existence for over 50 years. However, attachment theory has not yet developed a distinct therapeutic model. Instead, it has featured more as a research and assessment approach and has informed therapeutic approaches. In my view the recent move to the study of narratives in attachment theory does offer some extremely helpful directions for therapy. It may offer clinicians some helpful guidance to exploring how these can be combined into an attempt at a new integrative approach, that of ANT.

1 Attachment: meanings and identity

The chapter starts by suggesting that attachment theory offers important insights into how we develop a sense of who we are: identity and self. It suggests that attachment theory, though locating basic needs for attachment as biologically based, also offers a social account of how patterns of relating to others develop. The chapter reviews the basic concepts of attachment theory with an overview of the main attachment patterns that have been described. This is followed by an overview of the concept of 'internal working models' which show how the child learns to predict the availability of parents to offer protection from danger. It is suggested that working models can be seen in terms of the development of a system of meanings about self and others. The chapter then moves to a discussion of how the children learn to develop ways of managing their feelings with the help of their parents. The chapter ends by empha- sizing the interpersonal and systemic nature of attachment processes.

Speaking with Cathy

Int:	Can you describe your family in terms of relationships?
Cathy:	It's very false, it's very strange. I mean it's changed a lot. When I was younger it was just awful all the time, I don't like anger now, it's like, arguing non-stop. It was horrible. I would do anything to stop them arguing and anger is like fear. I don't like anger now, its like an emotion that can't be controlled and that scares me ... But recently everyone's been really trying but it still seems, it seems really false to me ... The only thing I ever hear them talking about is me and if I didn't have this [anorexia] it's kind of like, would everything fall apart, at least it's keeping them talking. And they won't argue while I've got this because it might make me worse. So um ... that's kind of bought, sort of like, I'm not in control as such but I've got more control over the situation that way.
Int:	So if you were upset or distressed or frightened when you were young, who would you go to?

> Cathy: Nobody. I wouldn't go to anybody. The only time I ever did was once when Mum was at work and I had to sleep in my brother's room. I can't remember why, and there was a picture of me and her when we were little, cuddling, and I was only young and I was looking at this picture and I was crying so much because I thought because they're older than most parents that she was going to die really soon and I went down to Dad and he was like 'Don't be stupid and go back to bed', and I had to go back to bed. And after that I didn't bother going to him. I would just bottle it all up and just not bother

Cathy (17 years old) was helping us with a piece of research exploring patterns of attachments in families. I had also worked with her and her family clinically during the time that they were struggling with anorexia. Here she was asked to comment on her life in her family, her parents' relationship, her problems with 'anorexia' and questions about her memories of being comforted when she was a child. In her answers we can gain a glimpse of how she is trying to make sense of her life in her family. She offers a poignant account of what it feels like for her to be entangled in a triangle of conflict between her parents. Cathy also expresses eloquently that she has to remain fragile in order to halt what she sees as the destructive anger between her parents. In the second quote she goes on to describe how she expects she will be looked after when she is upset, who she thinks she can turn to, or not as in this case. Importantly she mentions both of her parents and recounts how the memory of closeness and possible loss in the future had provoked a powerful experience of sadness prompting her to turn to her father for support. Her memory of his unavailability seems to represent an important turning point for Cathy in her story of her relationship with her father. The extract also highlights that though attachment theory has had a narrow focus, especially on the infant–mother dyad, attachments in families are multiple and complex. Arguably the dramatic changes in family life mean that children are increasingly likely to experience parenting from both parents, step-parents, grandparents, siblings and carers outside of the family. In this chapter we will review some of the core theory which is predominantly based on studies of dyads but hold in mind this complexity of attachments in families.

The areas of the questions that prompted Cathys' account are drawn from the Adult Attachment Interview (AAI) which we will look at more closely in Chapter 3. In this chapter we will look at the early development of attachments which start to occur before the child has language with which to express his or her thoughts. However, Cathy's account gives us an interesting insight into the experience and meanings of the early experiences that shape attachments.

Attachment theory and identity

I want to suggest in this chapter that attachment theory can be regarded as offering an important perspective on the development of self. This includes ideas about how the child develops an identity, an idea of who we are and how we came to be the way we are. This can be seen to fit with a social constructionist approach which emphasizes psychological theory and therapy as necessarily personal, subjective and concerned with the construction of meanings and identities. It may seem odd to pick attachment theory here since it has not typically been identified with a social constructionist stance. Instead, it has been seen as belonging firmly to a modernist approach which starts from a view of biological essentials and offers a typology of attachment styles and is, potentially, a position which is anathema to social constructionism.

I have struggled with how to start to talk about attachment theory without becoming entangled in what might seem like a modernist and reductionist approach. In particular it is very easy to become caught up in describing attachment styles, ways of reliably assessing these and descriptions of the actions of carers, especially mothers, who cause these. I want to suggest that there is value in exploring commonalities in how different patterns of self evolve but at the same time trying to connect with the unique meanings that people hold about their lives. This is why we have started by looking at Cathy's account to suggest both the commonalities and the uniqueness of her experiences.

What sense can we make of what Cathy is saying about herself and her family? One way of using an attachment theory lens might be to say that it indicates that she *has* a preoccupied attachment style in that she is caught up in her painful feelings and powerful memories come to mind as she remembers aspects of her childhood. Based on such a small set of extracts an allocation to a strategy is very difficult, not least since she is also apparently showing aspects of a *dismissive* strategy as she explains that her decision has been not to turn to anybody, to rely on herself. Describing her as *preoccupied* or *dismissive* implies that there is, residing inside her, an entity that can be classified and perhaps even measured. It belongs to a broadly positivist and reductionist approach which is interested in objective classification and reducing phenomena to basic entities. Another way to think about what Cathy is saying is to say that she is expressing or showing what attachment theory describes as her *working model* – an enduring set of beliefs or representations that she holds about her family and herself. These beliefs are seen as having a stability and reality which can be mapped and measured.

Yet another way of viewing Cathy's account is to see her as engaged in internal conversations – juxtaposing different ideas which show tensions in her thinking. This has been called a narrative or dialogic approach, which also considers that she is engaged in an act of contemplation about herself as she responds to the questions from an interviewer (Bruner 1990; Gergen 1999). This making sense appears to involve an active inner dialogue in which she draws out contrasts and tensions between different explanations, under-standings and feelings that she holds. For example, in describing the picture of her mother there is a tension between accepting that her mother is una-vailable and a longing for a closeness with her. Also, we can see a tension between wanting closeness, and pushing this feeling away and contemplating that she should only depend on herself. Cathy is also engaged in an inter-action in that she is talking to another human being – a female research psychologist some 20 years older than her – who is trying to make sense of what she is saying and Cathy is assisting her to do so. Cathy can be seen then as not simply describing her life and expressing her beliefs but as co-constructing a story with the researcher which makes sense to both of them.

Finally, in reading the quotes from Cathy we are making sense of them in terms of our own beliefs and experiences, and our own attachment patterns may play out in how we connect with her experiences. Are these different positions irreconcilable? Jackson (1957, 1965), one of the founders of sys-temic family therapy suggested that we should consider 'patterns' and com-monalties in families, not as realities but 'as if' – as propositions or hypotheses then we can usefully employ as ideas to guide our thinking and practice. Likewise, Bowlby (1969) initially suggested that it was best to hold a tentative view of the attachment patterns that he had observed. He suggested that it was premature and pejorative to give them names, such as avoidant or anxious/ambivalent until we knew more about what they meant, and instead suggested they simply be called A, B and C patterns. Unfortunately, his advice seems to have gone unheeded and attachment theory as a consequence has become widely seen as suggesting a judgemental approach, which may be unjustified.

Basics of attachment theory: biology and evolution

At the core of attachment theory is the proposition that we share with other species an evolutionary-based instinct to seek protection from a parent (or carer) when we experience danger. Based on observations of children who had experienced separations and losses, Bowlby (1969) first articulated his ideas about attachment theory in terms of the damaging effects that maternal deprivation could have on a child. He said that children in orphanages and other institutions who were separated from their parents, especially their mothers, could demonstrate emotionless or sociopathic identities. They seemed angry, aggressive, had difficulty showing intimate feelings and had difficulty in managing their relationships. Bowlby (1969) was profoundly interested in the developing identity of these young people and how many of them were coming to play roles in society of unhappy, delinquent outsiders and social outcasts. His descriptions were sympathetic to the distress of these young people who he described as trapped in ways of being that were distrustful, wary of others, prone to engaging in deceit and apparently lacking or unwilling to be able to empathize with other human beings' problems.

Bowlby (1969, 1988) argued that the infant is born with a repertoire of behaviours, such as crying and reaching for the parent, which are activated when the child is distressed or threatened:

> A central feature of my concept of parenting [is] the provision by both parents of a secure base from which a child or an adolescent can make sorties into the outside world and to which he can return knowing for sure that he will be welcomed when he gets there, nourished physically and emotionally, comforted if distressed, reassured if frightened. In essence this role is one of being available, ready to respond when called upon to encourage and perhaps to assist, but to intervene only when clearly necessary.
>
> (Bowlby 1988)

The development of attachment is especially important for the human infant, since it is a considerable time before we are able to move, feed or defend ourselves. It is important to emphasize that attachments relate to behaviours that are activated by threat and danger and not all interpersonal interactions.

Bowlby (1988) described attachment as an interactive system in that the sense of safety is maintained within tolerable or comfortable limits. When the infant feels relatively safe and unthreatened he or she is able to explore and venture away from the parents. This potentially exposes him or her to threat or danger which, if encountered, produces a distress response in the infant. The parent monitors the infant's explorations and responds to provide protection and safety if they become distressed, and in this way the child's emotional system returns to a comfortable or tolerable balance. Likewise, when the child seems content and safe the parent is able to give more of his or her attention to engage in other activities but not to the extent that this child's safety is neglected. Part of the parent's attention remains focused on what the infant is up to. As we know this continues into young adulthood, if not further. Middle-aged parents may breathe a sigh of relief that they can get on with their own lives when the child becomes more independent and eventually leaves home.

Bowlby (1969) argued that attachment is a fundamental, inherent biologically based motivation. He emphasized that attachment is inevitable and that children become attached to the parents or caregivers whether they provide reward or not. This is painfully evident with children who have been severely abused by their parents and may nevertheless remain strongly attached to them. Bowlby (1969) suggested that attachment operates as an adaptive self-regulating system and used the militaristic analogy of a heat-seeking missile which does not simply remain on a set course but is able to adjust its direction according to information about its target's location. So when a child is upset or frightened he or she will use a variety of means to gain proximity to the parent, such as crawling, walking or crying until picked up and comforted. Once calm and feeling safe he or she may start to explore the environment again (see Figure 1.1 below).

The attachment system as such is essentially 'in' the child and the parent or carer is the object of the child's attachment system. How the parent responds to the child's attempts to establish contact will come to shape the child's attachment system. These differing patterns of responding are seen as producing the child's attachments styles: secure, avoidant, anxious/ambivalent or severe/disorganized.

Attachment theory is predominantly concerned with safety and threat, and how these fundamental needs are met is seen as setting not only the

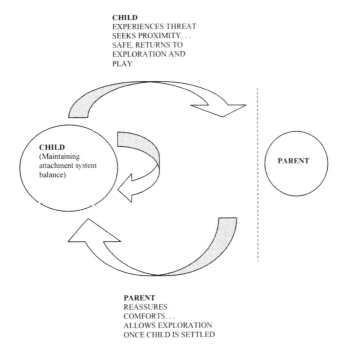

CHILD
EXPERIENCES THREAT
SEEKS PROXIMITY...
SAFE, RETURNS TO
EXPLORATION AND
PLAY

CHILD
(Maintaining
attachment system
balance)

PARENT

PARENT
REASSURES
COMFORTS...
ALLOWS EXPLORATION
ONCE CHILD IS SETTLED

Figure 1.1 Child's attachments as a system

current and immediate patterns but also as being generalized to other relationships. Hazan and Shaver (1987) suggest that these early patterns can be seen in later romantic relationships so that partners function as attachment objects for each other.

Though the early attachment relationship is described in terms of the child's biologically determined instinctive repertoire of behaviours it is important to note that the same may also be possible for the parents (see Figure 1.2).

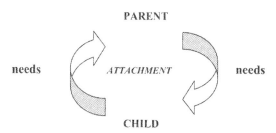

Figure 1.2 Attachment needs as mutual

Since Bowlby's (1969, 1973) initial observations of how children respond to separations there have been studies exploring how parents respond to their infants. For example, it has been shown that mothers appear to respond instinctively to different types of cries or distress in their infants and can experience distress and arousal in tune with their infants' states. Furthermore, it has been shown that early physical contact, touch and smiling, are extremely important for the mother to feel bonded to her infant. As the infant develops, this reciprocity of attachments will become more complex and subtle. Parents, for example, may feel bereft and very distressed themselves if they feel rejected and abandoned by their children.

Multiple Attachment Figures

Almost from its inception a crucial debate in attachment theory has been whether there is one primary attachment figure or whether there can be several. This also raises questions of how long the carers need to be involved, and what kind of care-giving they need to provide to function as attachment figures. With shifting patterns of family life and the greater involvement of fathers in providing care it has been argued that attachments are now more likely to be multiple. One view is that attachment figures can be seen as being in a hierarchy, with attachment figures varying in how important they are to the child (Bretherton 1985). As in Cathy's case we can see that she appears to be saying that her mother is more important for her and that she turned to her father when she was unavailable. There probably is no definitive answer to the question of whether there is invariably a primary figure. Howes (1999) suggests a number of important reasons for why it might be advantageous in survival terms for this to be the case. Having a primary figure means that at times of danger, there is less chance of confusion about who is responsible for the child. Likewise, the child is clear on who to turn to when in danger. In situations of serious threat or danger, time is of the essence so this may be an important issue. However, a number of studies suggest that when fathers take on early care-giving activities there are few differences between the child's attachment to them and to the mothers (Lamb 1977; Howes 1999). In situations where the mother is primarily involved early on, her attachment to the child appears to shape that of the father with the child (Steele and Fonagy 1995). Howes goes on to say, 'Fathers who express more positive feelings about their infants and their role as parents, and who assign a high priority to time spent with the infants, have more secure infants' (1999: 679).

Howes (1999) remarks on how there has been very little literature on grandparents as attachment figures. This is an interesting area and my clinical and personal experience suggests that grandparents may have an extremely important role as attachment figures, especially when parents are unavailable, ill, abusive or have abandoned a child.

Finally, there are many questions regarding the extent to which parents now employ childcare of various sorts so both parents can work. Howes (1999) makes the point that though this involves repeated separations for the child they also learn that the parent, most commonly the mother, also predictably returns and engages in pleasurable and comforting activities with the child. Of course there are situations where mothers have to work in poorly paid, exhausting conditions leaving little possibility for mutually constructive and pleasurable activities with their child.

Attachment patterns

Bowlby (1969), from his initial observations of children who had been separated from or had lost their parents, observed that they appeared to differ in how they were able to relate to people and express their feelings. His focus then turned to examining children who did have parents and he noted striking differences in how they responded to separations from their parents. He distinguished between patterns that seemed to him to suggest that the child was secure as opposed to insecure in his or her attachment to people. Bowlby initially identified three strikingly different patterns. He cautiously suggested that they be labelled A, B and C in order to avoid leaping to judgements about what the patterns meant. In the patterns that he saw as secure (B) the children would show distress and protest at separation from their parents, but could be comforted and reassured fairly rapidly, after which they could settle back into play and exploration. Children showing the insecure (A and C) patterns, on the other hand, tended to have more difficulty in being comforted and reassured, showing either a pattern of avoidance or a mixture of anxious, clingy and rejecting behaviours.

Bowlby also came to notice that even children who had not experienced prolonged separation from their parents could develop difficult emotional problems. This led him to be curious about the nature of the interactions in families and to attempt to identify what might be the source of children's anxieties. The exploration of such patterns was given significant impetus by one of Bowlby's students, Mary Ainsworth (Ainsworth et al. 1978), who developed a now widely used research protocol, the Strange Situation (an observational experiment, see Box 1.1 below). (Children in these studies typically ranged from between 2 to 5 years of age.)

Box 1.1 The Strange Situation

Mother and child interaction observed through one-way screen and video-taped in observation room:

- Mother and baby settle and interact: play with toys, etc.
- Stranger enters the room – minimal interaction with mother and baby
- Mother leaves for 3 minutes
- Mother returns and attempts to re-engage in play with baby
- Mother leaves again for 6 minutes
- Mother returns again and stranger leaves
- Mother attempts to re-engage in play with baby

Based on observations in the home and through these more structured and controlled observations in the Strange Situation Ainsworth confirmed that on reunion after a separation infants characteristically exhibited one of three main patterns: secure, avoidant or anxious/preoccupied (clingy) attachment styles (see Box 1.2 below). Mothers in the Strange Situation studies were seen to differ in how attuned they were to their babies' needs while engaged in play with them prior to the period of separation. For example, mothers of infants who showed secure patterns, on reunion appeared to be more attuned, sensitively responsive, non intrusive and synchronized with their children's actions and emotional responses. In contrast, mothers of infants who acted in insecure patterns on reunion were characteristically either more distracted and less attuned to their child or less predictably available (Ainsworth et al. 1978).

Box 1.2   Basic attachment patterns

Secure

Child quickly becomes calm when the parent returns, establishes eye contact and shows positive feelings. The interaction indicates that the parent is 'special' for the child who feels safe enough to return to play and exploration.

Insecure

Avoidant(A): Child acts cool and uninterested when the parent returns, 'as if' he or she does not care whether the parent is present or not and indicates that he or she did not miss the parent. Little attempt is made to contact the parent physically or verbally. Compulsive caring – child acts more like a parent than a child.

Ambivalent/Anxious (C): Child shows contradictory behaviour, shifting from being dependent and seeking comfort and crying to showing anger and resistance.

Severe (A/C): Child shows unusual and disconnected actions, freezing, incomplete movement towards the parent, confused, dazed expression and depressed feelings. Clinical population!

There is a debate within attachment theory regarding the classification of attachments, especially what is described above as Severe (A/C). This has variously been described as disorganized or as a 'cannot classify' category (Main and Solomon 1986). It was noted that on detailed analysis, for example using videotape of the Strange Situation interaction, some children displayed unusual or 'bizarre' behaviours which did not fit easily with any of the patterns. Sometimes the children appeared to freeze, show rigid, strange postures or express great distress, such as howling, and remaining inconsolable. Rather than seeing these as unclassifiable, Crittenden (1997) argues that they embody extreme versions of the A and C patterns and may be related to circumstances where children have experienced extreme early experiences, such as abuse, danger and further punishment and danger when they expressed fear or other negative emotions.

> 'He really laid into me, er it was his boot, it was his fists, er kickin' me, punching me all around the house ... And he'd say if you don't stop crying you're going to get another one ... [on another occasion] ... and I got another one and I don't know why I didn't cry'

In this short account from an adult looking back on his childhood we can perhaps see the kind of actions in his family that might have led him as a child to develop Severe A/C strategies. It seems that his expression of fear and distress as a result of a beating activated further beatings from his father. Such attacks may be extremely confusing and frightening for a child, especially as they come from a parent to whom he or she looks to for love, comfort and protection in times of dangers. For a young child to reconcile these contradictory experiences of extreme fear of and the need for love from the same person may be extremely confusing. 'Bizarre' behaviour, such as shifting between severely avoidant and highly fearful, anxious strategies, would make sense in such contradictory contexts. Other examples may be where a child is teased, ridiculed or humiliated for showing fear and vulnerability.

Attachment patterns and relationship with the parent

Observations of parents in the Strange Situation suggest important and characteristic differences in how they interact with their infants. These observations fit with a systemic perspective that emphasizes that the child's behaviour arises from the nature of the interaction with the parents. It is also important to note that as the patterns develop the parent's actions are in turn prompted by the child's actions. In effect as the patterns become established, should a parent wish to change the nature of the interaction with their child, it may not always be easy to do so. Though attachment theory tends to locate the attachment patterns in past sequences between child and parent it is possible to see this instead as an ongoing pattern whereby the behaviours are being maintained in the present interactional patterns (see Box 1.3).

Box 1.3 Relationships between attachment patterns and parent's behaviour	
Secure infants (B):	Rapid response to the baby's needs, mother offered more affectionate physical contact, tender and careful when holding the baby, more sensitive, attuned to the baby's needs
Avoidant infants (A):	Delayed in responding to infant's needs, less acknowledgement of baby, less responsive, tended to be abrupt and interfering and rejecting, expressed more anger and irritation, more likely to use forcible physical intervention to back up verbal comments
Preoccupied infants (C):	Delayed longest in responding to infant's distress, mothers tend to occupy themselves with routine activities while holding the baby, less responsive, tended to resist the baby's efforts to feed themselves, appeared more inept at handling the baby during close physical contact
Source: Ainsworth et al. 1978	

These classifications can have a judgemental quality and recent research suggests that these patterns of 'attachment' are complex (Cassidy, et al 2005). Critically, a parent can foster secure attachments by being 'good enough', for example even if he or she delays, ignores, is non-responsive to the infant, as long as a positive response eventually occurs, especially when the child needs reassurance and comfort. Importantly, also the parent does not intrude into the child's activity with their own fear or trauma. In short being 'good enough' has wide scope and is not about being a 'perfect', doting, self-sanctifying parent!

The findings are also summarized in Figure 1.3 below. As this figure suggests, there is a continual dynamic process between the parents and the child. Over time and many repetitions they accumulate into a set of predictions for the child about what he or she can expect to happen when distressed and frightened.

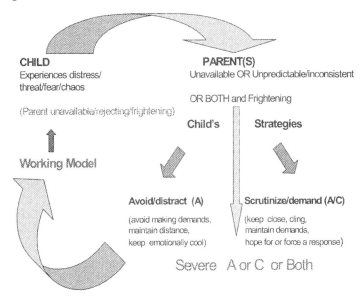

Figure 1.3   Attachment strategies and parental styles

Internal working models

Though attachment behaviour is seen to be motivated by biological and evolutionary processes from the outset, Bowlby (1969, 1988) also argued that these early experiences came to be constituted as mental processes. He chose the term 'working model' to capture the idea of a dynamic and active mental process. The child is not simply acquiring an internal memory of events but the working model is in some ways like a computer simulation programme that has stored information about events and then actively makes predictions based upon a model of the external world:

> Every situation we meet with in life is constructed in terms of the representational models we have of the world about us and ourselves. Information reaching us through our sense organs is selected and interpreted in terms of these models, its significance for us and for those we care for is evaluated in terms of them, and plans and actions conceived and executed with those models in mind. On how we interpret and evaluate each situation, moreover, turns also how we feel.
>
> (Bowlby 1980: 229)

The 'working model' includes a set of beliefs or expectations about others and the self in terms of:

- One's own and other people's behaviour
- Views of the self: how lovable, worthy and acceptable am I?
- How available and interested are others in me, and in caring for and looking after me?

In addition a child develops views about relationships and self in relation to, for example, her parents' relationships. In Cathy's case, she had a sense of herself in relation to the relationship between her parents. The parental relationship can constitute a context which is safe or one which elicits a sense of fear and anxiety.

Bowlby (1969) emphasized that the internal working models help a child to make predictions about his or her parents' likely responses and in turn to develop strategies to help him or her to deal with these. He distinguished between what infants do to meet their attachment needs – their *primary strategies* – and what they do if the attachment figure is not immediately available or the child's internal working model predicts that they will be unavailable or unpredictable – their *secondary attachment strategies*. If the child has experienced that a parent is unpredictable or inconsistent they may develop a *hyperactivating* strategy which may include closely monitoring the parent, increasing demands and insisting on contact. In contrast, if their expectation has been that the parent is reliably unavailable they may develop a *deactivating strategy* consisting of cutting off, not seeking contact, avoiding looking at the parent. Developmentally, young infants will initially be very distressed if not comforted and these strategies only come into play as the child starts to develop some capacitates for self-regulation.

In effect the child is seen as developing two types of strategies: one which attempts to shut down the attachment feelings and the other which escalates them. Both types of attachment patterns are regarded as consuming a considerable amount of mental energy, or epistemic space. Kobak (1999) has shown that despite appearing to be shut down children who show avoidant attachment patterns are nevertheless highly physiologically aroused. Likewise, young people who are anxious/preoccupied are also physiologically aroused. Their concern with monitoring others' availability possibly fits the pattern of distractedness observed in children with so called 'hyperactive' disorders. Crittenden (1997) has argued further that the deactivating strategy involves an emphasis on cognition and a variety of ways of distancing oneself from feelings, especially those relating to attachments.

One of the consequences of insecure attachments appears to be that children in both patterns have less space or spare mental capacity for accessing relevant emotional and cognitive information about relationships and for the complex task of integrating this information. Importantly it may also leave less space for them to engage in play, exploration and for contemplation of other people's thoughts and feelings. Fonagy et al. (1991a) refers to this capacity as 'reflective functioning', in other words, the ability to think about one's own and others' internal states. This has also been described as the development of empathy. More broadly, the child needs to develop abilities to integrate information about other people's intentions and situations, and his or her own feelings and thoughts. This also comes to involve a need to notice inconsistencies, contradictions and errors in one's own thinking.

Representation: cognitions and feelings

An important question is how the young infant makes sense or represents the early events in his or her life. Crittenden (1997) explains the early development of internal working models in terms of the child's ability to make sense of two types of information. The first is *cognitive* information whereby the infant learns that certain events follow others. For example, the infant may consistently experience that displaying distress leads to aversive consequences. Initially, as in conditioning, this can occur at a preconscious level. The young infant does not yet possess the schemas or language to be able to be consciously aware of these connections. The second type of information is *affective* or emotional. Infants instinctively experience emotions, such as fear, anxiety and distress triggered by various situations such as darkness, loud noise, unfamiliar surroundings and being alone. These feelings can be altered, if coupled with the presence, for example, of a parent who helps them, instead of being frightened, to feel reassured and comforted. Alternatively, the feelings can become more intense and associations can be made so that aspects of a situation which previously were not frightening can become coupled with or associated with the fear of danger or distress.

Crittenden (1997) argues that these two processes explain how the characteristic attachment styles develop. These representations give meaning to our interpersonal experiences. Importantly this represents a prediction of how a parent will react to our distress and fear.

Avoidant attachment style

It is argued that this strategy develops when a child repeatedly and predictably experiences that the parent is not available or that the child is rejected if he or she displays or tries to gain closeness. The child may learn that his or her cognitive information is reliable because it reliably predicts that their parents will be unrewarding or punitive regarding their displays of distress. Eventually this leads to a shutting down of display of feelings. The child evolves ways of distracting himself or herself from the need for attachments, such as by attending to non-personal aspects of situations. An extreme form of this can be a preoccupation with things rather than people, as in conditions described as Asperger's spectrum disorders. For example, young children may avoid looking at or interacting with the parent. Since this may be punished as being 'rude' when the child gets older, he or she may learn to engage in falsification, such as pretending to be happy when he or she is sad and distressed. Alternatively he or she may later engage in care-giving as opposed to care-seeking behaviour since this is more likely to be rewarded (Crittenden 1997).

This pattern is also described as *deactivating*, since attempts are made to shut down the emotional system. This pattern occurs when seeking support from others is seen as a non-viable option and attempts are made to reduce the risk of frustration or further distress from the attachment figure being unavailable. It is suggested that this strategy broadens to distancing oneself from any form of distress whether it is attachment related or not. It involves active inattention to threatening events and personal vulnerabilities as well as suppression of thoughts and memories that might evoke distress. If this feature of the strategy does not work, for example if a painful memory is unexpectedly aroused by association, then the thoughts are actively suppressed or repressed. Broadly the strategy also involves withdrawing from close relationships, suppression of painful negative memories, repression of negative memories, failure to acknowledge negative feelings and denial of basic fears. There is a development of a belief in the need for self-reliance which may encourage a denial of one's own vulnerabilities. In contrast to the hyperactivating strategies the person's internal world may be tidy and ordered but an emotional desert which is devoid of the clutter of feelings, needs, distress and other people.

Anxious/ambivalent attachment style

It is suggested that here the child's experience is that the parent is inconsistently available when he or she displays distress. The child may therefore maintain excessive displays of distress and emotion. This can also mean that other features of the environment may become associated with anxieties and fear as the child remains in a distressed state for extensive periods of time. In addition the child can be seen to be experiencing an intermittent reward pattern which effectively maintains this display of negative feelings. This pattern also prompts the child to become hypervigilant so as to maximize the possibility of any attention and care as soon as it appears to be available. In a context of uncertainty the child will be searching for cues as to when their needs may be met. Since this becomes almost impossible to predict the only reliable prediction becomes their own display of affect: 'If I am crying, demanding and angry eventually I will have my needs met'. However, the crying and demands may in turn be met by angry responses from the parent telling them to 'shut up', for example, which provoke further distress and anger in the child.

This strategy, also known as *hyperactivation*, may be associated with decreased exploration and play, excessive focus on and concern with the parent, alternating with displays of distress and anger. This involves an increase in the tendency to detect threat and danger, an increase in the intensity of emotional responses to threatening events and a heightening of mental ruminations on threat-related concerns. There is a self-amplifying process whereby the person is chronically preoccupied with possible signs of disapproval, waning interest or possible abandonment. With the advent of language, the internal dialogues are likely to be saturated with pessimistic views of the world, others and with possible negative outcomes. There may also be a negative view of the self, alternating with anger at others' imagined betrayals. Activation of attachment-related worries may occur even when there is no actual external threat:

> Hyperactivating strategies produce a self-amplifying cycle of distress in which chronic attachment-system activation interferes with engagement in non-attachment related activities and makes it likely that new sources of distress will mingle with old ones, thereby creating a chaotic and undifferentiated mental architecture
>
> (Mikulincer et al. 2003: 85)

Secure attachment style

Here the infant experiences a consistent response from the parents to provide comfort and reassurance as required. The infant is therefore able to predict the parents' behaviour cognitively and is also able to express his or her feelings. This allows the possibility for the infant progressively to become more able to use cognitive information to predict events and also to employ a wider repertoire of emotions including positive ones. It may also mean that he or she is able to regard situations as safe and be less distressed by new contexts.

His or her experience is likely to have been that any anxieties which may have been triggered by his or her exploration in new situations were consistently followed by receiving comfort from his or her parent.

Importantly both the insecure strategies imply that attachment needs continue to occupy a large part of the child's thinking and experience (Kobak and Cole 1994). In effect both types of strategy leave the child distracted by attachments and less available to engage in other activities. In particular, they are more likely to lead to the child being stuck inside a loop of continually striving to avoid or gain care.

A dynamic: developmental view

Crittenden (1997) argues that attachment should be seen as a dynamic, maturational process. The working models are the preliminary meaning systems that a child develops. They become increasingly complex and sophisticated as cognitive and language abilities develop. As suggested above the child develops not only a model of how others are likely to respond to their needs but also of themselves, for example, whether they are worthy of love and affection. This sense of self in relation to others is a central component of a developing identity. The avoidant pattern is characteristically associated with a sense that the self is not worthy of love and affection and that it is best not to expect to be looked after by others. There is a sense of not feeling good enough and minimizing the importance of attachments. In contrast the anxious/ambivalent pattern is associated with a sense that attachments and feelings are central and a fear both of rejection and of anger towards others for not providing the caring.

As the child develops so does the capacity for more sophisticated cognitive processes. In particular Crittenden argues that the working model features attempts to predict future events (see Figure 1.4 below).

This process of making meanings can come to include various processes whereby information is transformed, manipulated or even falsified. Discarding of information may occur when a child repeatedly experiences that feelings of desire for comfort are followed by rejection or punishments. In effect these feelings become extinguished or inhibited since they do not serve to gain what the child needs, namely comfort. On the other hand distortions may also occur as the child develops causal predictions of how likely events are to occur. Along with a discarding of information may be the development of generalizations, such as 'I will always be rejected', even though in reality the parents are available on 10 percent of occasions. However, the odds on rejection are so great that the child in effect distorts them to 'play safe' and avoid the prospect of hurtful rejection. A further process may be where the child comes to falsify meanings, for example, by learning that it is better to pretend to think or feel differently to how they really do feel.

DISCARDING: experience of certain types of information/experience being misleading. For example, desire for comfort --- > rejection; feeling uncomfortable -- > threat

DISTORTION: causal prediction is exaggerated. For example, I will *always* be rejected; my parents are *never* consistent

FALSIFICATION: Learning that it may be better to pretend to others and to myself that I feel or think differently to what I really do since doing this is less likely to lead to rejection. For example put on a happy face when I really feel sad and angry; lie to get what I want when parents do not keep promises

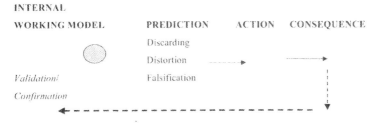

Figure 1.4 Prediction and development of attachment cognitions

Crittenden (1997) argues that the child develops increasingly more complex and sophisticated strategies with the maturation of the brain, complex reasoning and language. She argues specifically that language becomes one of the most easily falsifiable strategies so that we can say things that we do not mean or learn to deliberately distort interpretations of events or even talk about events that have not happened. She argues though that two overriding processes are in place: avoidant-dismissive patterns, whereby feelings are dismissed and cognitions are predominant and, in contrast, anxious/ambivalent, preoccupied patterns whereby feelings predominate and cognitions are shut down (summarized in Figure 1.5).

Crittenden's (1997) model moves beyond the classic four pattern model: secure, avoidant, anxious/ambivalent and disorganized. She argues that all attachment patterns are organized in the sense of having a fit with the interpersonal context of the child: these are the best ways that child can adapt to and make sense of his or her family situation. However, they have implications outside the family. For example, she argues that children in the C (preoccupied) patterns develop an increasingly split mixture of coercive and helpless strategies. These may develop, in the extreme, into paranoid and menacing strategies in which all actions, or even non-actions, even from strangers, are seen as potentially dangerous and threatening. These are likely to be children who have been severely frightened and exposed to high levels of inconsistency throughout their lives, typified by children in the care system. Likewise, at the extreme the high A (dismissive) strategies may involve very high levels of self-reliance; delusional beliefs, where, for example, parents who were quite abusive are seen as loving; or the child may try very hard to be what he or she feels the parents want him or her to be. It can also be

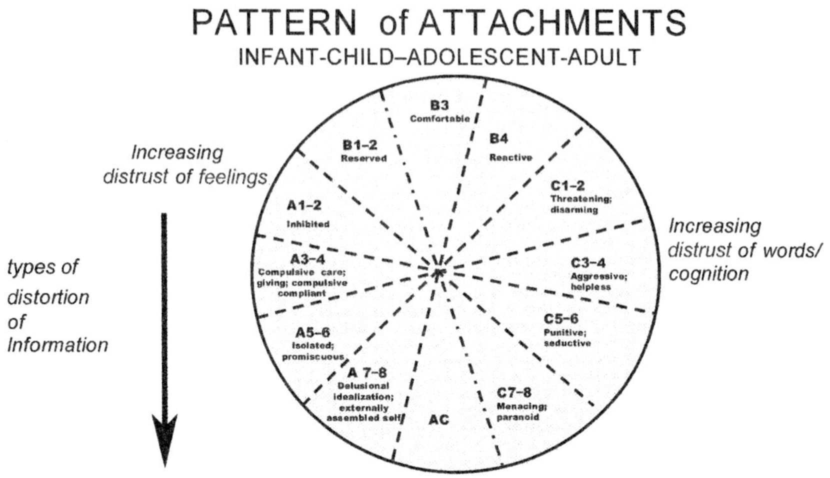

PATTERN of ATTACHMENTS
INFANT-CHILD–ADOLESCENT-ADULT

Figure 1.5 A dynamic: maturational model of attachment styles. Though shown as attachment styles or categories Crittenden's model can be seen as a dimensional approach – that these are tendencies on a continuum from increasing reliance on cognition or feelings and increasing distortion of information.

Source: Crittenden 1998

associated with a pattern of compulsive care-giving where the child tries to please and care for the parent in order to gain some small recognition and affection from them.

This model can also be seen to correspond with Bartholomew and Horowitz's (1991) two-dimensional model (see Table 1.1). These two dimensions feature avoidance and anxiety as central features of attachments. Secure attachments are seen to feature low avoidance and low anxiety – the person is able to turn to others for support and is not anxious about doing so. In contrast people who are highly anxious but not avoidant can be seen to be the anxious/ambivalent group in Main at al.'s (1985) classification. In addition this model differentiates between people who are avoidant but anxious and want close attachments, as opposed to those who dismiss the importance of

Table 1.1 Two-dimensional model of attachment

	Low anxiety	**High anxiety**
Low avoidance	Secure	Anxious Ambivalent
High avoidance	Dismissing Avoidant	Anxious Avoidant

attachments. Crittenden's mixed A/C classification can be seen to correspond with the anxious avoidant patterns in that they contain a mixture of both anxiety and avoidance. This is a dimensional model hence it is not restricted to the four usual attachment patterns.

An important feature of Crittenden's (1997) model is that it emphasizes the dialectical nature of the attachment strategies in which each variation is a mixture of at least two contrasting positions. This resembles George Kelly's (1955) personal constructs theory and object relations theory in terms of the development of self as consisting of contrasting positions. In addition it fits with a dialogic view of self as 'work in progress' – that we are in continual tensions of opposing internal processes or dialogues. Furthermore she argues that the strategies may also contain A–C combinations, for example, where an avoidant strategy in the face of massive emotional upheaval ceases to be viable for a child there may be a temporary reversion to an anxious/preoccupied strategy. This may also be revealed in particular aspects of experience such that there may be unresolved aspects of our experiences for which we revert to non-typical strategies. We will discuss this further in the following chapter when we look at the development of narratives in more detail.

Feelings and beliefs

It is interesting to consider how these strategies may influence the cognitions, stories and narratives that we hold. Pereg (2001), for example, suggests from a series of experimental studies that the attachment strategies influence how people react cognitively to negative and positive emotional experiences. For example, in one study participants were asked to read either a distressing account of a car accident or a neutral account of assembling a hobby kit. Following this induction of negative or neutral feelings the participants were then asked to read a booklet with a list of positive and negative headlines and then without prior warning were asked to remember as many as they could. In a second study they were asked to list the causes of a negative relationship event, such as 'your partner revealing something that you wanted them to keep secret'. Participants who had hyperactivating strategies (high attachment anxiety scores) remembered more negative headlines and saw the relationship problem in terms of more enduring and general causes. Participants with de-activating strategies were not influenced by the induced negative event. However, those with secure strategies remembered more positive headlines and saw the relationship problem in less enduring and general ways. Mikulincer et al (2003) suggest some important aspects of studies such as these:

> Importantly, the findings indicated that hyperactivating strategies ended up negatively biasing attributions about a relationship partner

even when the partner was not the source of the negative affect. That is, negative cognitions about a partner can be triggered not only when a partner behaves in a relationship-threatening manner but also when negative affect is elicited by other relationship-irrelevant sources

(Mikulincer et al. 2003: 88)

Such findings fit with much research and clinical evidence. For example, with domestic violence where an anxious partner appears to entertain negative and threatened thoughts with no apparent triggering action from their partner.

Equally interesting are findings relating to differences regarding the influence of positive emotional experiences. Mikulincer and Shefi (2000) suggest that attachment strategies can influence the extent to which people are able to engage in creative activity and cognitive activities. For example, a chronic focus on threat-related issues consistent with a hyperactivating strategy or the aversion to new and unsafe events in the de-activating strategies reduces people's opportunities to explore even when the environment is relatively safe. They found that the induction of positive feelings could enhance creative problem-solving for people classified as secure and had no effect on those classified as avoidant. Interestingly though, positive mood induction could reduce problem-solving for those classified as anxious-ambivalent.

Some interesting conclusions from such research are that those who have an avoidant, de-activating style appear to disregard both negative and positive feelings. Hence, they shut down the opportunity for developing an awareness of feelings. This contrasts with the anxious, hyperactivating people where either negative or positive feelings may activate negative feelings. There may be various reasons why this occurs, for example, positive feelings may start to turn into a reminder that in the past many positive feelings ended painfully. Again this fits with clinical experience where memories of more positive times can produce a release of distressing emotions. Partly this may also be about negative predictions about the future – a belief or story that their life will continue on its unhappy course. We can see this in part by turning back to Cathy's account at the start of the chapter. It is the picture of her and her mother being close which triggers sad feelings of possible loss in the future: 'and there was a picture of me and her when we were little, cuddling, and I was only young and I was looking at this picture and I was crying so much because I thought because they're older than most parents that she was going to die really soon'.

Managing feelings: from joint to self-regulation of feelings

Attachment-seeking behaviours are evident not only during childhood but during the whole of our lives. Attachment theory suggests that there are patterns for how children learn to expect to be looked after when they feel anxious or distressed. More broadly we can see this as the need we all have to rely on others for support and comfort in times not just of physical danger but also of emotional distress. As children develop these figures may become people outside of the immediate family: friends and later sexual partners and, increasingly perhaps for many people, counsellors and therapists.

The ability to use other people to manage our feelings of threat is synonymous with the attachment styles. Mikulincer et al. (2003) add that the child's developing working model comes to contain two aspects: declarative knowledge, which is about trust, a set of expectations about others' goodwill and about one's own ability to manage distress, and procedural knowledge, which concerns what the child is learning to do. It is seen to include the willingness to show fear and distress to others, seek support from others and engage in problem-solving to reduce the distress. Relatively secure people have learnt that acknowledging and displaying distress elicits support from others. They have also learnt that they can often cope themselves but turning to others can assist coping when necessary. Arguably there is a positive cycle inherent in this since these beliefs allow greater exploration, fun with others and, in turn, looking after others as well as being looked after. These help to build a sense of competence and trust and further develop the self-regulation capacities and a sense of autonomy. They are able to choose when to be autonomous and when to seek help. Unlike, for example, an avoidant attachment style they do not feel compelled to always try to resolve their distress alone. Cathy puts this poignantly, 'Nobody. I wouldn't go to anybody . . . I went down to Dad and he was like "Don't be stupid and go back to bed", and I had to go back to bed. And after that I didn't bother going to him. I would just bottle it all up and just not bother'. In her account there is also a broader sense that she has decided that the best strategy is to keep things to herself and not expect to turn to anybody.

From needing initially to rely largely on parents and carers to help manage their feelings, children become able to do this for themselves and to decide when and how to involve other people to help them when necessary. As we have seen earlier, a child develops secondary strategies when the actual attachment figure is not physically available and a part of this involves developing and turning to *internal representations* of our attachment figures:

As a person gains experience and develops cognitively, more and more of the role of a security enhancing attachment figure can be 'internalised' and become part of a personal strength and resilience. In adulthood, the question about literal attachment figures becomes transformed into a question about the adequacy of internal as well as external attachment-related resources for coping with stress. In many cases, internal resources are likely to be sufficient, but when they are not the person with a secure attachment history is willing and able to depend on actual attachment figures for support

(Mikulincer et al. 2003: 82–3)

Mikulincer et al. suggest that situations which are threatening, and this can include, for example, even the experience of reading threatening words, arouse attachment-related thoughts. In effect we seem to start to think about our attachment figures when we experience threat even of a mild level. They go on to suggest that the roles of our attachment figures become internalized and we come to apply to our self what we remember the attachment figure having done in the past. This may mean that we can imagine what they would do in this situation themselves and what they do or say to make us feel better.

Shaver and Mikulincer (2002) suggest that children proceed from co-regulation of their feelings to being able to manage some of them themselves by three related processes. The first is through exploration. As the child learns that it is safe to venture out into the world they are exposed to new experiences and may learn that they can manage on their own and even that they are able to assist others with their feelings. The second process is described as an expansion of the self. When an adult comforts the child their responses are

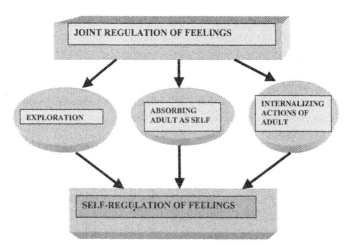

Figure 1.6 Processes in developing self-regulation of feelings

synchronized with the child's needs. This can foster a feeling of contact, of being joined and experiencing the adult as part of oneself. The strengths and competencies of the adult are in this way incorporated into a sense of the self. This might include how the parent is emotionally, how they set about solving problems and what they say. Finally, it is suggested that the child is also able to internalize or mirror the actions of the adult, for example how they compliment, approve and celebrate the child's actions and successes. The child can come to imagine or replay in their minds what a parent or other adult figure would say to them. When these three processes occur positively the child may be able to develop in confidence and in ability to regulate their own feelings.

But what happens when these three processes do not occur in a constructive manner? Mikulincer et al. (2003) outline a possible phenomenological account suggesting that a child may experience two different kinds of mental pain: one resulting from a frustration of one's attachment needs and failure to remain close to the attachment figure. The second is a sense that we are unable to work together with the attachment figure in dealing with distress and anxiety. In the first state of mind closeness to the attachment figure is experienced as non-rewarding or even punishing, so the child becomes afraid of punishment in the future should they seek attention. The parent may engage in various behaviours that foster this feeling: consistent inattention, threats of punishment for showing negative feelings, traumatic abusive experiences when the child seeks closeness, explicit or implicit messages that encourage self-reliance and prohibit the expression of neediness or vulnerability. Rather than a source of comfort, the attachment figure, and proximity to them, may become the main sources of threat. Here the child comes to feel that they can only regulate their feelings alone and cannot rely on others.

In contrast Mikulincer et al. argue that a different state of mind develops when the child experiences inconsistency and intrusiveness which leave him or her helpless and vulnerable, and so the child responds by trying harder to gain the protection and comfort they need from the attachment figure. In this case distance from the attachment figure is experienced as distressing. The behaviours of the caregiver here may include inconsistency, intrusiveness and blocking of autonomy, explicit or implicit messages emphasizing the child's incompetence, vulnerability and helplessness and traumatic or abusive experiences when the child is separated from the attachment figure. The prospect of managing their feelings on their own is therefore experienced as frightening and they feel helpless and alone. In this case the child is likely to feel that they cannot possibly manage on their own, that they are helpless but also angry if the parent is unavailable to help sort their feelings out for them.

Mikulincer et al. (2003) are able to offer interesting connections between descriptions of the child's internal experiences – a phenomenological per-spective – and the patterns of actions they evolve as strategies to manage their feelings and, especially, to deal with their need for comfort and reassurance.

This chapter has explored the development of attachment in terms of the child's identity and sense of self. It has been suggested that how the child comes to evaluate herself, especially in terms of, 'am I worthy of love' and 'can I rely on others to look after me' is central to an emerging identity. Intrinsic to this developing sense of self is how a child gains the abilities and the confidence to manage their own feelings along with being able, and willing to call on others to help her to do so. Importantly, this views attachment and identity as social, inter-personal processes. The next chapter continues this theme with an exploration of attachment and communica-tional processes in families.

2 Systems, communication and attachments

This chapter explores the links between systemic perspectives and attachment theory. It overviews the systemic basis of attachments theory and how Bowlby formulated attachment as an interactive system in which child and parent mutually regulate each other's behaviours and feelings. The communicational basis of systems theory will be discussed with an analysis of attachment and internal working models as communicational processes. This features a discussion of the openness of communication in the relationship system. This can be seen as a set of 'rules' about what emotions and events may be communicated and also the development of communication or narrative skills. Using an attachment as communicational framework the chapter takes another look at double-bind theory and how this is fuelled by attachment anxieties. The chapter moves on to explore couples' relationships and considers how attachments to romantic partners resemble and may be influenced by childhood attachments. It then progresses to an exploration of more complex family patterns, namely triangles and how the parental dynamics can provide a context of security or lack of it for the child. Finally, the chapter concludes with a look at how the child may become entangled in the parents' marital conflicts and serve to regulate the emotional distance between them.

As we saw in the previous chapter the concept of attachment has been described as an instinctive process which fulfils an evolutionary survival function for the infant and in turn for the species. Bowlby (1969) had employed ideas from systems theory to explain the nature of attachment patterns but essentially this was an intrapsychic rather than interpersonal version of systemic thinking. He did recognize though that as a child developed he or she also comes to influence the parents' actions and feelings.

Systems theory

Systemic approaches emphasize that any human interaction is characterized by a process of mutual influence which is based upon feedback. This has also been described as a circular view of causations as contrasted to a linear process (see Figure 2.1).

Comforts

Nancy ⟶ Daniel ⟶ *Settles and stops crying*

Figure 2.1 Linear pattern

In a linear process the causation is essentially one-way, the influence Nancy exerts on her child, Daniel. However, this can in fact be seen as a circular process when we examine it in detail since the comforting is not simply a one-off event, it may occur over a period of time and may influence both child and mother. In some cases it might take a considerable period of time for Nancy to discover what is causing Daniel's distress and how to soothe and calm him. In this way the comforting can be seen as a circular pattern, as being interactive, whereby the mother and child are mutually influencing each other (see Figure 2.2).

Offers comfort: talking
touching, reassuring, smiling

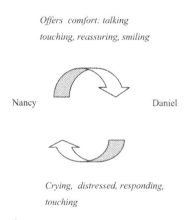

Nancy   Daniel

Crying, distressed, responding,
touching

Figure 2.2 Circular pattern

Attachment theory has been extremely valuable in illuminating how a parent and child may engage in different patterns of caring (Ainsworth 1973). It is possible to map the two main insecure attachment patterns as systemic patterns regulated by feedback between child and parents. In addition to being able to depict these as interactional patterns it is also possible to see how these at the same time are asssociated with the shaping of two organizations of internal states – the suppression of feelings or cognition (see Figure 2.3).

In the anxious/ambivalent patterns the child initially is seen as encountering unpredictable responses from the parents. Consequently the negative feelings escalate and the child continues to protest and demand. As the child matures these behaviours may become increasingly coercive and threatening and the parents may come to feel that they have to give in and

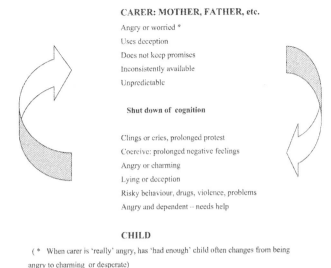

CARER: MOTHER, FATHER, etc.

Angry or worried *
Uses deception
Does not keep promises
Inconsistently available
Unpredictable

Shut down of cognition

Clings or cries, prolonged protest
Coercive: prolonged negative feelings
Angry or charming
Lying or deception
Risky behaviour, drugs, violence, problems
Angry and dependent – needs help

CHILD

(* When carer is 'really' angry, has 'had enough' child often changes from being
angry to charming or desperate)

Figure 2.3   Anxious/ambivalent parent–child pattern: escalation

often come to feel powerless. On the other hand, the parents may at the same time foster a sense of helplessness in the child by intrusive care and by fostering a sense of dependency. Hence, when the parents angrily withdraw this can in turn create a huge sense of rejection, anxiety and a helpless response from the child. In effect both parents and child become caught in a highly emotionally charged interactional process from which it becomes increasingly difficult to become disentangled.

It also becomes increasingly difficult to make sense of the situation – to employ cognition, since feelings predominate and inconsistency prevents causal, temporal sequences being identified, apart from the fact that feelings and negativity will arise. It is typical to hear parents in this sequence speak of the impossibility of making any sense of what is going on or of developing any coherent strategies: 'There is nothing we can do, nothing seems to work, we can't understand why she is like it'. As the child matures he or she becomes increasingly able to use deliberate manipulations, not just to be angry but to be angry deliberately and to use coercion. Furthermore other strategies such as lying and deception become likely since he or she cannot count on the parents behaving consistently or keeping their promises, and cannot trust what has been said. It is also likely that children find it difficult to be able to understand why their parents behave as they do since talking is usually imbued with feelings and quickly escalates out of control. The parents may also use deception tactics, for example distracting the child in some play before sneaking away as a way of avoiding upsetting the child. With an older child they may feel they have to be deceptive or even lie in order to avoid the

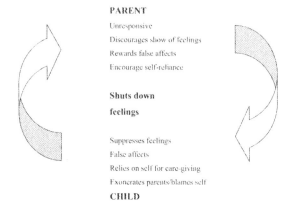

PARENT

Unresponsive
Discourages show of feelings
Rewards false affects
Encourage self-reliance

Shuts down

feelings

Suppresses feelings
False affects
Relies on self for care-giving
Exonerates parents/blames self

CHILD

Figure 2.4 Avoidant parent–child pattern: escalation

constant emotional eruptions and arguments. This all adds to an inter-personal context in which words and cognitions come not to be trusted and emotions and outbursts predominate (see Figure 2.4).

In contrast in the avoidant patterns there is an over-reliance on cognition. The parents are very predictable for the child and there is a very clear message that expression of feelings is unacceptable. As this pattern progresses the child may develop other strategies, such as a reversal of caring, where instead of being cared for by the parents the child becomes a carer for the parents. Parents may respond with some acknowledgement of this which the child can construe as an expression of affection, though in fact the child had prompted a response by the caring in the first place. Children may also develop patterns of falsifying their feelings and of becoming increasingly self-reliant. As children become older they may find other ways of pleasing others, for example in offering sexual favours or engaging in relationships but deliberately concealing their feelings.

These two representations of the avoidant and anxious/ambivalent patterns suggest that the patterns can be seen as based upon mutual influence and feedback. The patterns can be seen in terms of short-term interactions but also as progressing over longer periods of time: years as opposed to minutes.

Punctuation

A further contribution that a systemic perspective can make to our understanding of attachment patterns can be seen in the idea of punctuation (Watzlawick et al. 1967; Procter 1981; Dallos 1991; Eron and Lund 1993). This suggests that patterns of interactions can be seen in terms of interconnected cycles of construing and action: our beliefs lead us to act in certain ways and the consequent feedback from our interactional partner can in turn reinforce our beliefs. This pattern can then be similarly experienced by the interactional partner (see Figure 2.5).

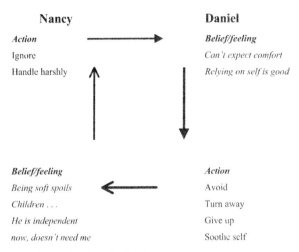

Figure 2.5 A circularity of actions–beliefs/feelings

Though the above is clearly a simplification it does illustrate the possibility that attachment patterns may develop from such feedback loops of actions, beliefs and feelings. One way of recognizing that this is a mutually maintained pattern is if either partner attempts to change it. Nancy might at some point feel that she would like a little more affection from Daniel but since he is convinced that she is pretty tough and has learnt a belief in self-reliance he is unlikely to respond to her invitation. Likewise, Nancy is unlikely to respond to Daniel becoming more affectionate or showing his needs, were he able to do this, since this might convince her that he is still too clingy and soft.

Escalation

A systemic view emphasizes that without some form of stabilizing process such a cycle would escalate so that the pair would become extremely disengaged. However, it is possible that Nancy initially had some ideas about an acceptable level of 'softness' in children and that her relationship with Daniel has stabilized around a level such that if their relationship veered too far either side of what is acceptable for her some adjustment would take place. Crittenden (1997) describes this in her model in terms of attachment patterns which show gradations of dismissive or preoccupied styles (see fig. 1.5). This in turn relates to the extremity of the parental behaviour to the child in the first place. Phenomenologically perhaps such an analysis is best illustrated by the desperation that parents can come to feel in their relationship with the child. For example, parents of children displaying extreme anxious/ambivalent patterns can feel victims of the pattern of tantrums, coercive behaviour, threats and seductive behaviour from their children. At the same time they are often very unaware of the inconsistencies in their own actions towards the child that maintain such patterns.

Systemic approaches here have also emphasized that dyads can be seen to escalate in two patterns: complementarity – where the partners display different but complementary behaviours, for example the child is the dependent and the parents are the carers; and symmetry – where both partners display similar behaviours. Both patterns are prone to escalation. Though initially the parent–child pattern can be seen as complementary as the child learns the attachment style of the parent, it may become symmetrical. For example, Nancy and Daniel (see Figure 2.5) both demonstrate avoidant behaviour. In theory all attachments should therefore become symmetrical, that is the child acting in the same way as the parent, since the parent is initially shaping the child's behaviour. However, though there is evidence that there is such transmission across the generations the correspondence between parents' and child's patterns is not complete. Research suggests that there is a considerable amount of variability across the generations (Crittenden 1997; Salomon and George 1999). As we will consider later in this chapter, this may in part be because attachment is a multi-person rather than essentially a dyadic phenomenon. Likewise, system theory came to suggest that the processes in dyads were essentially unstable and needed the input of a third person or others to help stabilize the process. It may likewise be the case that we need to consider attachments as being at least a three- rather than a two-person process.

Attachment theory shows similarities with systemic perspectives in that stable patterns were seen to consist of flexible alternation between processes whereby the interaction could move between symmetrical and complementary patterns. Likewise, as the infant receives the care and reassurance they seek they start to become calmer and divert their attention to play and exploration, decreasing the demands on the carer. The interaction can turn to a mutually symmetrical one whereby carer and child both enjoy and stimulate each other with smiles, laughter and play. As children develop the relationship can also shift between symmetrical and complementary patterns with the child at times entering into a caring role, such as when a parent is ill or upset. Where this does not become chronic it can be appropriate, because the child is learning to take important steps towards competence and independence. The carer in such an interaction can become more relaxed and direct their attention to other activities.

However, attachment theory has had much less to say about what is happening to parents, for example how they experience the infant's demands, how they perceive their own actions with the infant, how competent or how overwhelmed they feel. Observational studies of parents' behaviour in the home situation (Ainsworth 1973) suggest that parents do have distinct styles of interpreting and reacting to their children's demands, but there are few studies exploring this.

> I consider it unfortunate that studies of attachment relations as experienced and represented by the attachment figure are almost non-existent. Even when adults' internal working models of attachment relationships have been examined, investigators were interested in them only in terms of the adult's childhood experiences with parents. The failure to study the parental attachment system, including parents' internal working models of attachment relationships, is a serious shortcoming of attachment theory
>
> (Bretherton 1985: 33–4)

So extending a systemic analysis to the infant–parent dyad suggests that the child shapes and is not just shaped by the process. Some aspects of such a mutual process has also been explored in terms of, for example, infants' temperament. Some babies are more active than others, some more easily frightened and distressed and so on, and this may impact on the mother's responses (Belsky 1999; Vaugh and Bost 1999).

In addition it is important to take a developmental perspective. As the child develops his or her ability to influence the parent increases greatly. Older children start to be able to make more overt demands, to comment on the parent's behaviour and criticize in various ways. These actions impact on the parent and influence how they feel about themselves. Also, children's success, failure, anxieties and painful experiences outside the family impact on the parents. Perhaps one of the more typical scenarios for family therapists working with young families is that parents feel they are failing, inadequate and are not good enough parents. Attachment theory appears to suggest that parents who have secure attachments can weather these difficulties and that they are resilient enough not to sink into patterns of avoiding their children's needs or of becoming overwhelmed and unhelpfully entangled in their children's worries. However, this might be asking a lot of parents in some situations. A systemic perspective suggests that there is considerable scope for difficulties to arise prompted by a variety of external factors which can steer a secure parent towards an insecure attachment with a particular child. Attachment does appear to suggest a somewhat linear process whereby the parent shapes the child rather than vice versa. Salomon and George (1999) suggest that a more systemic, circular view is possible: 'It is likely that the influence of the baby on the care-giving system is part of a feedback loop; in other words, it is transactional rather than linear and unidirectional' (1999: 659). Perhaps an interesting research question here is whether family therapy which aims to change the characteristics of the family system, including the interactional pattern between the parent and child, and within this the child as well as parent, can lead to a shift towards a more secure attachment classification in both parents and child.

In agreement with the emphasis on viewing attachment as a systemic process George and Solomon (1999) argue that there is a need in attachment theory to explore not only the development of attachment styles and internal working models in infants but also to examine such changes in the carer. An influential perspective in attachment theory has been that the quality of care that parents, especially mothers, provide is directly related to their own attachment styles. We will explore this in some detail in the next chapter but essentially the argument is that the mother has acquired a working model of attachment from her own experiences as a child with her own parents and this becomes activated and shapes how she reacts towards her own infant. A key feature of this, it is argued, is how sensitive the mother is, or how attuned she is to the needs of her own infant. Attachment theorists have suggested that under normal circumstances, a mother integrates her experiences with her child into her mental schemas of attachment (Bretherton 1985; Main et al. 1985; Fonagy et al. 1996). The evidence for this view has been on the basis of mothers' attachment representations as predictive of the quality of the attachments with their infants. A key feature of this process is seen to be a mother's sensitivity to her infant and it has been suggested that this will override other factors, such as temperamental differences. Salomon and George, (1999) however, argue that the evidence is less clear than had been believed and that concordance between the mother's attachment style and the baby's is highest for mothers who are secure but is less convincing for mothers of insecure infants, especially when mothers are unresolved about early loss. One possibility is that mothers who have secure patterns may be in relationships which have the greatest level of consistency. Insecure patterns may also be associated with greater variability and inconsistency between the parents, making it less easy to predict which type of insecure pattern the child may develop. It may also be that in some cases the affection she experiences from a child may shift an insecure mother's pattern. This in turn impacts on the nature of the interaction with the infant and in turn shapes the nature of the attachment that takes place.

Later in this chapter we will explore how attachment theory has been applied to explorations of dynamics in couples. Adult relationships are more likely to be symmetrical in that each partner both provides and receives care from the other. There are of course variations such that in some relationships one partner is in a dependent role and the other is the carer, for example in cases of illness of one partner, differences in age or emotional dynamics. Also, as we have mentioned earlier, as children grow and mature their ability to impact on the caregiver increases, possibly even to the point of being able to alter the caregiver's attachment style. Bretherton (1985) puts this forcefully:

> Some might say that we ought to study the caregiver–child relationship as one system. It is, of course, true that an attachment relationship – or any relationship, for that matter – is the joint work of two persons (achieved within the framework of a particular family and a particular culture). In this sense it is appropriate to consider the caregiver–infant relationship as a system ... However ... the two partners have, in a sense, two relationships: the relationship as mentally represented by the attached person and by the attachment figure.
>
> (Bretherton 1985: 34)

Attachments as communications?

Systemic family therapy was fundamentally a communicational theory approach. The early innovators (Watzlawick et al. 1967; Bateson 1972; Haley 1976) drew on ideas from cybernetics which emphasized systems as regulated by feedback, which in human systems was equated to communication. Watzlawick et al. (1967) suggested a broad view of communication which included language, non-verbal actions, gestures and even the idea that silence can be seen as a communicative act. Their dictum became that in human relationships, 'it is impossible not to communicate'.

Levels of communication

It was suggested that communication is invariably multi-faceted, such that any piece of communication necessarily consists of simultaneous layers of meanings. An important distinction was drawn between verbal and non-verbal communication. Specifically it was suggested that the verbal aspect of speech was seen as essentially conveying information and content in contrast to the non-verbal features, which were seen as communicating information about feelings and defining the nature of the relationships.

Conscious or unconscious communication

Communication was also seen to occur at both a conscious and an unconscious level. This fits with a developmental perspective in recognizing that communication is initially non-verbal and unconscious, and gradually starts to come under conscious control as language develops. As we grow older we become capable of consciously rehearsing and planning what we want to say and what effect we want this to have. However, we will invariably communicate at non-verbal levels as well and these are much harder to manage or manipulate (Gottman 1979, 1982). When we are interacting and in conversation much of our verbal communication processing also arguably takes place at a non-conscious or semi-conscious level as we enter into the ebb and flow of a conversation, especially if it is heated or animated.

Co-construction in communication

Communication invariably involves a 'sender' and a 'receiver'. This idea fits with a social constructionist perspective which emphasizes communication as a co-constructive process. In some instances the message we intend may not be the one that is received, such as when we feel that what we meant to say has been misconstrued and the received meaning of our communication becomes apparent when see how our listener has responded. Striking examples may be when we have unintentionally said something 'funny' or in the response from our listener we realize that we have communicated something more profound than we may have intended. Also, in communicational exchanges we convey how we feel and this may be jointly shaped. The emotional responses of our listener may escalate or diffuse our own feelings. Their responses can give a meaning to our own feelings of which we may not be fully aware. For example, a listener might explicitly make a comment such as, 'You seem very passionate about this,' or more subtly their non-verbal response may communicate that this is a dangerous topic or that you are 'over-reacting' or 'that I am a bit crazy'. The emotional levels can rise and flow in the communicational process so that we may feel elated or drained during or following a conversation.

Incongruity in communication

Such an analysis of communications is important in terms of developmental perspectives and attachment theory since the parent–child communication is initially non-verbal. Importantly it also draws our attention to the possibility that communication is complex and may be confusing. A range of studies have in fact shown that children rely more on the non-verbal features of communication and that this emphasis on 'how' people say things as opposed to 'what' they say continues into aspects of adult relationships, especially romantic attachments (Haley 1976). As these communicational studies developed it became apparent that incongruities could develop not just between communication levels but also within levels, for example, when a parent hugs a child in a cursory or dismissive way. Verbal communication itself contains non-verbal or paralinguistic features, such as tone of voice, hesitation, rapidity of speech and loudness, which also convey meanings. Systemic family therapy can attempt to clarify communicational processes, for example in relation to what was intended and incongruities between verbal and non-verbal aspects.

Double-binding communication

A particular form of incongruity in communication was suggested by Bateson (1972; Haley 1976) as underlying the development of serious mental disturbance. As an example of this process he described the following as illustrative of the pattern: a mother goes to greet her son in hospital. As he opens his arms and walks towards her she visibly stiffens. Recognizing this signal he hesitates and lowers his arms, whereupon she asks, 'Don't you love me any more?' The young man blushes and fidgets and his mother adds, 'You should not be embarrassed to show your feelings'. His mother here can be seen to offer an incongruous communication – the stiffening of her body communicates rejection and yet verbally she is asking for a show of affection. However, an important additional layer is that the child's attempts to react to this incongruity is then identified by her as wrong and also given a negative implication ('Don't you love me any more?'). He seems to be trying to understand and respond as best he can to the messages that are being communicated but either way he is put in the wrong. When he then blushes this in turn is criticized as a fault of weakness ('You should not be embarrassed to show your feelings').

The experience of such communication might be confusing, frustrating and anger-provoking. The young man was not showing his mother that he did not love her, he was responding appropriately to her non-verbal communication – her stiffness. But then this appropriate reaction was interpreted by his mother as being wrong. In his confusion he blushed which then provided a verification that perhaps he was wrong. The sense of confusion, feeling, 'Hold on, this is all wrong', may have been difficult to unscramble, especially as he was becoming frustrated and perhaps angry. Bateson (1972) emphasized that a significant feature of such interactions is that the child feels he or she cannot escape from the relationship. For this young man to shout and get angry at his mother was not appropriate, and also he didn't want to lose her love. However, he did become very angry when his mother left and 'had to be restrained'.

An attachment perspective underscores that this son needed the relationship and his fear of losing it was anxiety-provoking. The young man was in a psychiatric hospital, itself an anxiety-provoking situation which would naturally arouse his attachment needs, possibly including both feelings of rejection, abandonment and anger but also fear and anxiety. A sense of feeling rejected by his mother could therefore be an even more devastating feeling in this context. Hence, despite possible mixed feelings, he found it difficult to extricate himself. One solution, it has been argued, for young people who repeatedly experience this pattern is to withdraw into illness. This can permit an escape from the situation, but in a way which does not threaten the parent. Bateson (1972) also described that the mother in this situation was anxious herself and so was at the same time communicating vulnerability to her child, so it is very difficult for him to express anger directly towards her. Crittenden (2004) has described similar patterns of incongruity in her studies employing the Strange Situation where, for example, a mother may mock her child's communications of distress but then act as if she had not done this and 'really cares'.

Meta-communication

One of the ways of dealing with confusions such as in the process above is to meta-communicate – to talk about talk. Examples of this are when people offer clarification of their intended communication. This usually occurs when there has been some recognition that the listener has responded in a way that was not intended. For example, we may say things like, 'That is not what I meant', 'Oh, that sounds like I was suggesting . . .' Meta-communication can also be in the form of an invitation from us to the speaker for clarification: 'Sorry, what did you mean by that?' Or reflexive clarifications, 'What do you think that I meant?' Meta-comunication is a vital feature of open communication, especially as it helps to clarify intentions and how people are feeling. It may be blocked in situations which appear dangerous or where we feel disempowered. For example, a child may avoid asking a parent what they mean or what they are feeling for fear of punishment or ridicule.

A number of attachment researchers (Oppenheim and Waters 1985; Bretherton 1995; Crittenden 1995) have pointed out that assessments of attachment invariably require communication. The infant in the Strange Situation may communicate to his or her parent that he or she is distressed and angry. Alternatively he or she may at first sight appear to communicate that he or she did not really miss the parent and is perfectly alright on his or her own. Likewise, in an adult attachment interview the person being interviewed is involved in communicating to the interviewer experiences from their childhood. It has been suggested that difficulties in communication occur as a process of 'defensive exclusion'. Material that is too painful is seen to be excluded from the child's awareness so he or she is unable to communicate about it, except perhaps indirectly.

It can be argued instead that attachment and communication are synonymous and Bowlby (1988) has suggested this when he emphasized the importance of open communication for secure attachment:

> the striking differences in which [parent–child] communication is
> either free or restricted [are] of great relevance for understanding why
> one child develops healthily and another becomes disturbed ... the
> degree of freedom of communication in the pairs destined to develop
> a secure pattern of attachment is far greater than it is in those who do
> not
>
> (Bowlby 1988: 131)

The ability to communicate freely about positive and negative feelings is the
cornerstone of secure attachment. Following on from the discussion of affect
regulation in the previous chapter, it is clear that a child needs to be able to
clearly and openly express how she feels to her parents in order for them to be
able to help her manage her feelings. Likewise, the parents need themselves to
clearly communicate that this open expression of feelings is acceptable, that
they are willing to help and for them to give congruent as opposed to
incongruent messages about this.

Communication as a skill

It is suggested that the child's internal working model consists of a set of
understandings or predictions about how others will act and about the child's
own self. Linked to this understanding of self and others are ideas about what
is permitted to communicate about and how this is done. At one level this can
be expectations or family rules about what topics are legitimate to discuss, for
example whether it is permitted to talk about private body parts or sexual
matters. In addition to prescriptions about topics it is possible that the child is
also shaped in terms of the development of ability to communicate. Arguably,
an infant learns from his or her parents about communication and how to do
it. Expression of basic feelings such as fear, anger, hunger and so on may be
instinctive but even expression of these feelings are shaped by how the parents
respond. For example, they may learn not to communicate fear and worry if
this is predictably ignored or punished by their parents. In effect the child
learns not only that the parents are emotionally unavailable but correspond-
ingly that it serves no purpose to communicate these feelings. We might even
ponder whether we can see attachment not simply or predominantly as being
about the internal structure of people's feelings, but rather as how they have
learnt to express these feelings. Furthermore, from our discussion about levels
of communication above we can see that it is a sophisticated and complex
process. How does a child learn to separate out the layers of meaning and
possible contradictions between verbal and non-verbal messages?
　　Oppenheim and Waters (1985) emphasize that parents need to provide
the emotional 'scaffolding' – emotional safety and support – to help infants to

make sense of complex and negative situations. It is possible that playing games and even forms of teasing and joking assist children to discriminate between subtle communicational cues. Communication involves the twin processes of being able to decode, in other words to understand others' communications, and to organize one's own feelings and experiences to convey to another person what we feel, think, need and so on. In this process communication and perception are interwoven. So it is necessary to see 'internal working models' as both shaping and being shaped by communicational processes. How able a child is to express his or her needs and feelings will shape the responses of others and in turn serve to shape and maintain the internal working model.

Attachment styles linked to communicational patterns

The different parenting styles that are seen to shape attachment styles can be seen as affecting communicational styles. Secure attachments can be seen to result from family contexts where communication about positive and negative events is encouraged and the child is assisted in communicating what he or she wants, needs and feels. A variety of studies have emphasized 'atunement' or 'sensitivity' on the part of the caregiver as an important feature of communicational patterns and this can be seen as communicational sensitivity. The parent attempts to find out what the child needs and feels, and in this encourages rather than suppresses the child's attempt to communicate. This process can be seen as *scaffolding*, in that the parents assist and support the child's attempts to communicate by prompts, enquiry, offering examples and helping her to complete her communication. For example, a parent may enquire how the child feels, make some suggestions about what he or she might be feeling, help the child put the feeling into words and prompt him or her to extend or elaborate. However, these prompts and suggestions are offered in a tentative way which allows the child to agree or disagree. The emotional tone of the communication would need to be positive, focused and calm, to help the child to think and integrate ideas.

By contrast, in avoidant patterns the parents attempt to shut down expression of feelings, worries and fears. They communicate that the child must overcome these problems by him/herself and not to expect help from the parents. Moreover the parents may demonstrate to the child that communication is about a logical, rational analysis of situations and should be free of emotional tone and gestures. This means that over time the child is learning to keep emotions out of her communication in terms of both the content and the non-verbal features of communication. Since emotions are not being communicated the child does not learn how to talk about them or how to communicate with others to help them feel better. The child learns that he/she should not engage in emotional talk and consequently this may eventually become an alien territory for her. The child may come to feel stupid, clumsy, inept in talking about these things and hold back for this reason. However, under great distress the feelings may erupt in over-emotional outbursts about which the child may later feel ashamed or embarrassed.

The anxious ambivalent attachment patterns by contrast may be characterized by a lot of communication about feelings. However, it is likely that the communication here, in contrast to in avoidant patterns, contains less semantic information to anchor the feelings. In addition the parents may themselves alternate rapidly in their own feelings, leading to a confusion about what a particular event means or without any sense of consistency. Ainsworth (1973) and others have also described how the parents in the anxious/ambivalent pattern can communicate in an intrusive manner, for example, where the child is told, perhaps angrily or tearfully, that he or she is bad and wants to upset his or her mother. Through such communication the parent imputes negative internal states and intentions to the child. The child in turn may be swept along by the emotions, or feel angry at being misunderstood, and hence join in an emotive communicational process. Characteristically young children in these patterns have been described as engaging in violent tantrums and later coercive manipulative forms of communication.

Deception and distortion

As a child develops the range and complexity of his or her communication increases. With the advent of language it becomes possible not only to communicate but to engage in deliberate, strategic and even deceptive communication (Crittenden 1997). Bowlby (1988) proposed that a particularly damaging process for children was a communicational context in which a child's accurate perception of painful events is distorted or contradicted. He described a situation where a child who had witnessed the suicide of a parent had been subsequently pressurized by the surviving parent to believe and say that in fact the parent had died as a result of an illness. The communicational strategies involved in this kind of situation are likely to be scorn, ridicule or insisting that the child was confusing the real event with what he or she had seen on television or in a bad dream. Such an analysis of family processes has also been offered by Laing (1966) and early systemic therapists (Bateson 1972; Watzlawick et al. 1974). Frequently in instances of sexual abuse children are told that the abuse did not happen, that they imagined the abuse or that it was their fault. They may also be told very explicitly not to talk to anyone about the abuse. Such manipulations and distortions serve not only to block communication about the painful events but also to stunt children's abilities to communicate about issues surrounding the events.

Developmental processes and communication

Crittenden (1995) suggests that as children develop they become able to engage in more subtle communicational processes:

Preschool years

As the child develops through this period the ability to employ language increases and the child becomes more able to employ more sophisticated non-verbal communication. For the avoidant patterns the primary communicational process is the inhibiting of expression of negative affects. This can move the child towards the use of deception, for example the use of false displays of positive feeling when the child is feeling sad, angry or frightened. The child may learn from his or her parents not only that he or she must not show negative feelings otherwise he or she may be punished, but also that he or she may be rewarded for showing positive feelings that they do not feel. This has been called 'false affect' (Crittenden 1995) and can become a communicational pattern which the child then carries into adult relationships. Crittenden argues that in part the child is learning that it is 'rude' to show avoidant behaviour such as turning his or her back on parents or ignoring people, so the child learns to inhibit negative feelings and, importantly, learns that he or she should communicate positive feelings whether they are felt or not. Two further types of communication are seen to emerge: in serious neglect children may learn to display caring behaviour, and in cases of harsh treatment and abuse the child may learn to communicate in an extremely compliant, servile manner. He or she learns not to communicate any evidence of distress. Children who are in the anxious, preoccupied classification, on the other hand, learn to use exaggerated angry communications, including aggressive and overly avoidant behaviour. The purpose of such communication is to draw the parents' attention to themselves. In turn if the attention they receive is that of anger they may then employ 'coy' communication to disarm and so distract the parents from their anger. Crittenden (1995) argues that the communicational pattern can escalate so that the demands for attention can include threats and the disarming behaviour can turn into feigned helplessness. Deceptive processes can become endemic to the communicational process, for example the parents may use strategies such as deceiving a child into becoming interested in a toy in order to slip away unnoticed. From such interactions the child may learn that he or she must stay constantly vigilant and not trust what people say. The communicational patterns in the family tend to be endless unresolvable fights, conflicts and cycles of accusations and blaming.

School years

As children's abilities develop further they are able to employ their memory systems and mental processes to create more complex working models. One feature of this in avoidant patterns is that children may notice that they remember events and situations differently from their parents, and so they believe they should not remember the events as they do, or at all, in order not to incur the displeasure, criticism or even attack of their parents. In effect the parents communicate to them that it is better if the children remember events by borrowing the memories from the parents or that they do not talk about the events at all. In other words, they are required to follow 'the party line' and to talk only about the acceptable family version of events. Children who are in anxious-avoidant attachment systems, in contrast, increasingly experience the contradictions in the parents' communications, for example oscillations from, 'You're a bad boy' to, 'You're a good boy'; 'Didn't I tell you to ask permission?' to 'Can't you do anything for yourself?'

However, children learn that communication through exaggeration of their feelings can more predictably get a response from their parents. Their interest and communication remain very much focused on conversations with their parents about their feelings and so they appear to be excessively preoccupied with feelings and relationships, to the exclusion of the outside world and other interests. This can mean that they have little experience of non-emotive communication on other areas of interest, which makes it difficult for them to interact with peers, apart from, for example, 'winding people up' and getting into trouble at school in ways characteristic in extreme forms of 'attention disorders'.

Adolescence and adulthood

As children move into adolescence they develop abilities to engage in complex, abstract thinking. This includes forming perceptions of their parents in terms of distinguishing between them; predicting the likely effects of behaving in certain ways; discriminating between contexts to predict when and where they are likely to act in certain ways and what their internal states are likely to be, why they act as they do and how the parents see them. Linked to this is recognition of their own internal states and how they are seen by others. So a young person within an avoidant pattern may recognize that they typically damp down their feelings. One young man we worked with said, 'I know people think I don't care because I don't show my feelings. But I do care, it's just that I don't like and want to have to show them'.

In effect the question of choice becomes more central and, by contrast, anxious ambivalent patterns may be concerned with a recognition that they do exaggerate their feelings and decide when it is to their advantage to do so and when it is not. It is not simply that adolescents and adults choose how they communicate but rather that they may be more able to do so. Also, this choosing can be seen as shaped by the earlier underlying processes that are in place so that emotional and semantic material is filtered for the purposes of choosing what we communicate about and how we do this. In this choice it appears that people showing dismissive patterns will communicate, for example, that they are responsible for their actions and that the parents were justified in treating them as they did, that, as in the quote above, it is their choice to be as they are. By contrast the ambivalent/anxious pattern involves remembering past grievances and engaging in communication with parents which accuses and blames them for what has happened and so is self-exonerating.

Overall this analysis, especially Crittenden's (1995) work, suggests that communicational processes are likely to show consistency in the patterns throughout children's development. Importantly, the ability to use the strategies deliberately increases, including the capacity to engage in deception and falsification. However, extensive use and reliance on the latter is more likely to be a feature of the insecure attachment patterns.

Adult attachments

It is widely assumed that adult attachments, for example romantic relationships, are shaped by early childhood attachment experiences. Freud (1961) suggested that the infant–mother relationship serves as the 'prototype' for later adult romantic relationships. Attachment theory as we have seen suggests that the internal working models formed through childhood serve to shape our expectations of others and of ourselves. This in turn can be seen to shape our choice of partners and how secure our relationships become. Immediately a question arises of whether this is in terms of the choices we make in our selection of partners or how the relationships become constructed. Most importantly it raises the issue that, unlike the infant–parent relationship, adult romantic relationships are much more likely to be symmetrical, with a greater degree of mutual influence. It is possible that each partner's attachment style serves to shape their relationship but also that in turn the relationship may, over time, come to alter their attachment style. Certainly many clients report that an unhappy relationship has left them feeling bad about themselves, insecure, vulnerable or wanting to withdraw and give up on relationships.

The prototype hypothesis is further complicated by the fact that people experience a variety of attachment relationships during their lives. In childhood this may include relationships with mother, father, siblings, grandparents, non-family caregivers, teachers and other relatives. From adolescence onwards it may include romantic partners and spouses. How do all of these relationships add up? Do they lead to general, overall patterns that then shape all romantic relationships? Or, do subsequent romantic relationships each develop different attachment patterns?

Hazan and Shaver (1987) suggested that romantic love was an attachment process that resembled the way in which the infant becomes attached to its parent. They argued that the same three attachment styles, secure, avoidant and anxious-ambivalent, exist in adulthood and colour the ways that adults experience love relationships. People who have a secure attachment style from their childhood were seen to view their lovers as trustworthy friends. Anxious-ambivalent adults are more likely to fall in love at first sight and then long for their partners to reciprocate this, and avoidant adults were least likely to accept their partners' faults. They devised a set of descriptive statements, corresponding to attachment styles, which required people to chose which best matched the way they felt. Initially this was a three-way grouping but it was extended to separate out two types of avoidant patterns – fearful and dismissing (from Bartholomew and Horowitz 1991: 244):

- *Secure*: It is easy for me to become emotionally close to others. I am comfortable depending on others and having others depend on me. I don't worry about being alone or having others not accept me.
- *Dismissing*: I am comfortable without close emotional relationships. It is very important to me to feel independent and self-sufficient, and I prefer not to depend on others or have others depend on me.
- *Preoccupied*: I want to be completely emotionally intimate with others, but often I find that others are reluctant to get as close as I would like. I am comfortable being without close relationships, but I sometimes worry that others don't value me as much as I value them.
- *Fearful*: I am uncomfortable getting close to others. I want emotionally close relationships, but I find it difficult to trust others completely, or to depend on them. I worry that I will be hurt if I allow myself to become too close to others.

These studies generally suggested that there were links between attachments developed in childhood and people's romantic attachments. However, the measures used tended to be a non-specific appraisal of romantic attachments in general. For example, the instrument above was used in many studies so that people are asked to choose which of the above statements best characterized their view of intimate relationships. This choice was then correlated with measures of their childhood attachment styles and family histories. Some studies have also explored the relationship between these attachment patterns and sexual behaviour. For example, it has been suggested that adults employ sexual fantasy and behaviour to regulate their anxieties, such as fantasizing about, and engaging in, non-intimate sex with casual partners. People with avoidant patterns were discovered to use this to help maintain a 'safe' emotional distance from romantic partners (Simpson and Gangestad 1991).

In contrast Owens et al. (1995) conducted a study in which they explored the links between attachments as measured by the adult attachment interview (AAI) (see Chapter 3), which offers a very sensitive and detailed measure of childhood attachments, and they developed a similar in-depth current relationship interview (CRI) which assessed how attached the person felt to their current relationship. The interview consists of questions about their parents' marriage as well as their own relationship, for example in terms of issues such as loving, rejecting and being open. The analysis is in terms of anger, derogation of the partner and of attachment in general, idealization of the partner, passive speech, fear of losing the partner and overall coherence. Using this more sophisticated measure they found that 64 per cent of their sample of 45 couples scored the same on the AAI as on the CRI. It also indicated that partners did not significantly choose partners with the same childhood attachment patterns as their own. However, there was a very high correlation in terms of their current relationship attachment. This was seen as suggesting two possible interpretations: 'One, that people seek out (or stay with) romantic partners whose working models of adult love relationships are similar to their own and, the other, that, over the course of time, the partners' working models of their shared relationship converge' (Owens et al. 1995: 226).

Systemic processes

A difficulty with much of the research has been that it has assumed that attachment is a trait-like quality, that it is *in* the person and that characteristics of the person or the context of the relationship are not very important. However, partners typically report that their partner and their relationship can significantly alter not only how they come to feel about the specific relationship they are in, but also about relationships in general and also how they come to feel about themselves. This suggests that attachments in relationships are, at least in part, a product of the interplay between the partner's characteristics and the relationship's dynamics. Research by Owens at al. (1995) supports this view and also shows the extent to which partners' current relationship attachment is significantly related to their partner's childhood attachment pattern. So, each partner's representation of their own childhood attachment seemed to influence how attached their partner was to them. This suggests a co-constructional process in that the attachment to the partner is not simply a result of the person's own attachment style. However, they also found that this was influential, such that if the partner held a secure childhood attachment style they seemed more able to form a secure relationship attachment with someone who was also secure. People showing insecure patterns, however, were generally less able to develop a secure relationship attachment even if their partner's childhood attachment style was secure.

Some of the issues are illustrated by a study by Feeney (2003) which employed a content analysis of couples' relationship experiences. She found that nearly a quarter of her sample of 72 couples mentioned negative views of relationships based on previous family and romantic partners. Two-thirds of these partners mentioned that their current relationship had helped them to revise these models to be more secure. In some cases partners clearly described how they felt that the relationship could alter their relationship attachments for the better:

> I've never been one to get deeply into relationships. I never have with my partners before, even if they wanted to. But my current partner has always been especially keen, and showed a lot of interest, a lot of affection, a lot of love, and would do anything for me. So months down the track, I started to respond to all this; I tried to reciprocate the positive feelings coming from him, and opened up to him
>
> (Feeney 2003: 153)

Conversely, some participants also described how the current relationship was serving to erode a sense of security. For example, a description of a partner who saw herself as insecure describes how the relationship exacerbated this feeling:

> During this relationship, especially, I've often felt separate from my partner. He doesn't tell me how he feels about me and I'm naturally insecure, so I worry about it. Often, when I've felt this sort of anxiety he hasn't even realised. Sometimes he's self-absorbed, and doesn't seem to care what I want. I feel bad when he doesn't listen to me or take an active interest in my life. But I don't open up much about it very much, because I don't like conflict
>
> (Feeney 2003: 154)

Couples, attachments and triangles

We have seen so far in this chapter that the child can have more than one attachment figure and likewise adults may have multiple attachments, not

infrequently multiple romantic attachments. In fact a whole genre of literature and romantic fiction might be missing without the phenomenon of
complex attachments! As we have moved to a consideration of adult
attachments this has also raised the issue that attachment continues
throughout life. Almost since its inception systemic family therapy has
emphasized that a child's experience and development, and the development
of problems, is shaped by how the parents' relationship impacts on the child.
In particular family therapists have emphasized the child's involvement in
the parents' dynamics, for example being conscripted to take sides with one
against the other. In moving to a triadic analysis we can start to consider not
only the relationships that each individual has with each other person but
also how each person relates to the relationship between the other two and
even how each person experiences the triangle of the three individuals
together. We can therefore consider children as being in a triangle in two
ways: the attachment styles that are generated from their relationship to each
parent, and then in terms of the child's attachment to the relationship
between the parents. The latter concerns for example how safe children feel
when they are together with both parents.

Different attachments to each parent

A number of studies (Lamb 1977; Main and Weston 1981) have shown that
children do not necessarily, or even typically, have the same attachment
patterns to each of their parents. The question then arises:

> What happens to the internal working model of the self when a child
> feels secure in the relationship with one parent and not with the
> other? Which of these relationships is the one carried forward into
> other relationships, or are both carried forward in different types of
> relationships? Or are these the wrong questions to ask?
> (Bretherton 1985: 29)

It is a frequent observation in clinical work that people display different
attachment patterns towards different members of their family. In turn the
nature of these relationships often appears to be linked to the attachments that
they describe as having had with their own parents. For example, a father
displayed a harsh attitude towards his son, like the attachment he had with his
own father. In contrast, at the same time, he was warm and affectionate with
his wife, a pattern which he apparently carried forward from his relationship
with his mother. In this case it seemed that two attachment models were
operating side by side. Bretherton (1985, 1995) discusses this in terms of the
development of the complexity of internal working models. In some ways

similar to Kelly's (1955) notion of a construct system, the child may hold different constellations of beliefs about different people in his or her life. Attachment theory adds that each of these constellations in turn has a different affective component. (We shall return to this question in the next chapter.)

A second question concerns the way in which children are influenced by the relationship between their parents. A number of studies indicate that children who see violence and argument in the home between their parents develop pessimistic views about relationships. Such an effect is even indicated in experimental studies where children watched short video sequences of couples engaged in either amicable or negative conflictual interaction (Davies and Cummings 1998). The children who saw the negative vignettes were more likely to predict an unhappy and conflict-ridden future for the couple. Extrapolating from such studies it would follow that children who repeatedly experience conflict between their parents will develop more pessimistic views. Related to this, children were found more likely to say that they felt sad and predicted that they would be sad in the future following the viewing of the conflictual video sequences (of adults interacting). Furthermore, children who had experienced considerable conflict between their parents had lower self-esteem and self-efficacy. The effects are also evident in how children react to conflictual situations outside of the home. The negative experience of seeing their parents in conflict seems to prime children to be more emotionally responsive to adult anger. Davies and Cummings (1998) go on to describe that relatively minor incidents can set off strong feelings in people who have had such experiences and they are less able to regulate or manage the feelings. Some specific patterns have been identified, for example, where parents compete for control and for the child's attention and undermine each other's parenting. This appears to be associated with children developing impulse-control problems. Alternatively, where one partner withdraws and the other becomes very enmeshed with the child, this appears to be associated with problems in coping with anxiety (Haley 1987; Katz and Gottman 1996; McConnell and Kerig 1999). Children's attentional abilities have also been found to be linked to parental processes, as where parents who do not cooperate the children are likely to develop avoidant patterns of resistance to discussing family conflicts. In contrast children who had witnessed conflicts tended to be more preoccupied with these issues.

A further important area has been that of children's ability to understand the different family roles. At about age 5 or 6 children can start to understand that the person who is mother to them can also be spouse to their father. They can develop more sophisticated and qualified ideas about roles, for example following a divorce, they can understand that though Dad is still married to Mum he can withdraw from being her husband and still be a dad to me. Also, that he can stay emotionally close to me even if he has ceased to be so to Mum. Research by Watson and Fischer (1993) suggested that children aged 5 whose parents had divorced, compared to children in intact families, found it harder to see how their parents could continue to be parents if they were no longer married to each other, and that both parents could still love them though they did not love each other. Interestingly the researchers argued that an interaction between children's, as yet unlimited, ability to understand complex family roles and the distress of the divorce with the fear of losing one or other parent may exacerbate their difficulties in distinguishing between the parental and marital roles. Related to this, the process of separating the roles is easier for the child if each parent clearly stays close to them and endorses the other parent's role with the child. Failing to do this and allowing marital hostility to disrupt parenting is likely to confuse the child so that they are less able to discriminate between the roles: 'such children ... may fall prey to the painful conviction that their only options within the family are to side with one parent, intervene to resolve their parent's conflict, or withdraw from the family triad altogether' (Talbot and McHale 2003: 51).

It is possible that children who have been embroiled in family conflicts, for example with competitive parents, may come to believe that such conflict will spread and engulf everyone. Hence they may find conflicts in relationships difficult in later life, so that they feel inordinately responsible to step in and keep peace among people around them (possibly developing on a trajectory to becoming psychotherapists and family therapists?).

Distance regulation

One way of describing the processes whereby a child becomes entangled, as above, is the notion of the child becoming involved as a regulator of the emotional climate between the parents. Byng-Hall (1980) has suggested that couples can be seen as developing a level of intimacy that is in some way acceptable for them. A core concept in systemic theory has been that perversely this level can be very painful and uncomfortable yet despite this the relationship appears to stay stuck at this level. For couples who are relatively secure this can mean that they are able to tolerate periods of both closeness and distance between them, and furthermore that they are able to communicate relatively clearly about this to resolve problems before they escalate. In contrast, when the relationship has become insecure then it is the ability to communicate clearly and effectively to manage closeness and comfort that becomes problematic. This can mean that the couple live in a state of continual anxiety, tension, anger and mistrust. Such states are prone to escalation and then the couple's children are likely to become distressed by the conflict between the parents. In turn the children's distress may serve to distract the parents from their conflicts with each other (see Figure 2.6).

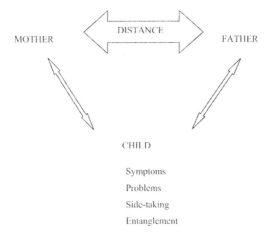

Figure 2.6 A child as distance regulator

This is the classic situation of conflict-detouring described by Minuchin et al. (1978) but Byng-Hall (1980) adds that it serves to manage the emotional distance between the parents. Another powerful example is where a child becomes so distressed that he or she can only sleep in bed with the mother. This can serve to regulate unwelcome sexual contact from the father but without this being explicitly stated by the mother.

This chapter has explored some important connections between attachment theory and systemic perspectives. In particular it has been argued that attachment can be seen not just as an intrapersonal phenomenon but as forming patterns or rules regarding communication in family systems. In the next chapter we will develop this idea by looking at how both the content and the organization of narratives are in turn shaped by the attachment processes.

3 Narratives and attachments

This chapter will explore further the concept of internal working models. It will discuss the idea that as the child develops the working model becomes more complex, especially with the onset of language. A number of concepts, such as schemas, generalized internal representations and scripts which have been employed to discuss the nature of the internal working model, are discussed. Ideas such as scripts theory and hierarchically organized schema systems are also discussed. Some tentative connections are also made to George Kelly's personal construct theory. The chapter then moves to developments in attachment theory which have employed narrative assessments, such as story stems and the adult attachment interview. These emphasize not only the content of the narratives but their organization as reflecting attachment patterns. This work is discussed with links to narrative therapy and theory which likewise emphasizes the concept coherence in the organization of the narratives. Links are made to developmental narrative research, which has also examined differences in the organization of children's narratives and how these correspond to different parenting practices. The discussion connects with the emphasis on attachment as communication in the previous chapter. The chapter ends by pointing towards implications for narrative and other forms of therapy.

Internal working models: further considerations

Bowlby's (1969) notion of the child as developing an internal working model sets the scene for attachment theory as an approach that could offer a valuable developmental perspective of how the child's internal world evolves in the social context of his or her family life. In this chapter we will continue the discussion in the previous chapter to look more closely at the concept of the internal working model and go on to suggest that developments in cognitive and developmental psychology, especially the emphasis on narrative as a fundamental feature of human experience, fits very well with attachment theory's turn towards a representational approach (Main et al. 1985).

From the outset Bowlby (1969) has emphasized that attachment behaviour, though essentially an instinctual biological survival system that connects children to their parents for their own safety protection, is also importantly a system of meanings that develops in sophistication as the child matures. In this section I want to pick up two important issues before the chapter moves to an exploration of attachment narratives. Narrative is itself a complex concept and it may be helpful to explore some of the components and building blocks of narrative, such as schemas, beliefs and scripts. The two issues or questions concern how a child's internal working model deals with two important problems that may arise: first, when the child experiences competing, contradictory and incongruous messages from and within the same parent; second, when the child experiences similar contradictory messages between the two parents or carers. Both of these situations are familiar for family therapists and other clinicians. Bretherton (1985) writes that the concept of the internal working model was drawn from the work of Craik (1943):

> If the organism carries a small-scale model of external reality and its own possible actions within its head, it is able to try out various alternatives, conclude which is the best of them, react to future situations before they arise, utilise the knowledge of past events in dealing with the present and future, and in every way to react in a much fuller, safer and more competent manner to the emergencies which face it
>
> (Craig 1943: 61)

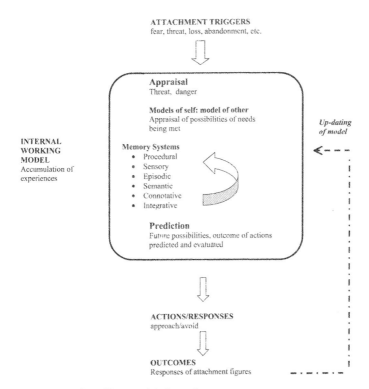

Figure 3.1   Internal working model of attachment

The working model implies a dynamic process which allows prediction to occur and also suggests that the person is involved in a constructive process – actively making sense of reality. It also suggests that once established the working model may operate outside conscious awareness and, though needing to be revised with new information, it also has a stability. New information and events are likely to be assimilated into the model and dramatic change may be disturbing and painful. This view of a working model resonates with George Kelly's (1955) idea of a personal construct system. Like Kelly's model it is argued that the working model needs to adapt and integrate new information – it needs to be open to revision and elaboration. It is also suggested that the model is initially based on the child–parent dyadic experiences. Importantly, the view is also shared that the construction of experiences is dialectical. For example, a child learns not only that a parent may be rejecting but also that the child is not worthy of love and comfort (see Figure 3.2).

Figure 3.2 Child–parent dyadic experiences

This again resonates with Kelly's (1955) personal construct theory and cognitive analytical therapy (CAT) both of which share the idea that our experience is composed of bipolar positions or constructs. The child here is learning both sides of the constructs and learns the role of being rejecting as well as being rejected. This 'reciprocal role' may later be turned towards others or towards the self. More benignly a child who experiences a relationship of trust and support from his or her parents learns about receiving emotional support as well as giving it to others (see Figure 3.3).

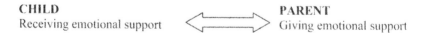

Figure 3.3 Relationship of trust and support between child and parent

Belief systems: the organization of working models

There have been a variety of suggestions regarding how the child's internal working model develops and is organized. A child needs to make sense of his or her attachment relationship with each parent, other members of the family and also his or her relationship to the relationship between the parents. The child can be seen as developing a representation of what people have done in the past – this includes memories in the form of episodes and with this ideas or hypotheses about how these people are likely to act in the future. Along with this there is a perception of the attachment figure and of the self. One idea that contains these features is that of a script. Through the repeated experience of interactions we are able to build up a generalized picture of what is likely to happen. For example, a child may come to develop a script of what happens at bedtime: drinks, bath, story, kiss and so on. More broadly we can see basic scripts operating in everyday life, for example the sequences of behaviour in a restaurant, in a shop or at a lecture. These are rather formal scripts and there are also scripts which are more flexible and propositional. Even young children at age 3 can provide a simple script, such as when eating dinner. Initially the scripts are likely to be local and specific and consist essentially of generalizations of episodic memories. Interestingly, children are unlikely to recall specific details of episodes unless they were somehow unusual or dramatic. So, when asked to remember dinner-time, what they are likely to remember is a generalized dinner-time script rather than a specific episode. Cognitively it makes sense to reduce mundane events in this way rather than to carry unnecessary detail of every event.

Bretherton (1985) also suggests that 'it may be useful to think of the internal working model of the self and attachment figures as a multilayered hierarchical network of representations'. He goes on to suggest that this idea fits with Epstein's (1973, 1980) self-theory and with the work of Schank (1982), which suggests that the working model consists of major and minor schemas/scripts.

In Figure 3.4 the basic level event schemas are generalizations based on how the mother usually acts when the child is hurt or upset. These can be connected to specific episodes or to memories of when she acted in this way.

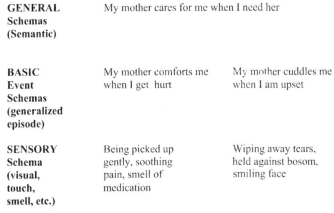

GENERAL Schemas (Semantic)	My mother cares for me when I need her	
BASIC Event Schemas (generalized episode)	My mother comforts me when I get hurt	My mother cuddles me when I am upset
SENSORY Schema (visual, touch, smell, etc.)	Being picked up gently, soothing pain, smell of medication	Wiping away tears, held against bosom, smiling face

Figure 3.4 A child's internal working model towards the mother

	SELF	OTHER
Core Schema	*I am reasonably OK and loveable*	*My parents react differently when I need them but by and large they both care in their different ways*
General Schemas (Semantic)	My mother cares for me when I need her	My father is somewhat distant
Basic Event Schemas (generalized episodes)	My mother comforts me when I get hurt My mother cuddles me when I am upset	My father ignores me when I am upset My father laughs when I get hurt
Sensory Schema (visual, touch, smell, etc.)	Being picked up gently, soothing pain, smell of medication, wiping away tears, held against bosom, smiling face	Gruff laughter, Dad reading the paper, making a joke of my injury, pat on the head, dad winking at me, feeling foolish

Figure 3.5 A child's internal working model – increasingly complex

At the next level of generalization these form into higher order attachment generalizations.

The child's internal working model is more complex than this since it will also contain ideas about the father and other members of the family, and later on a whole range of people. Figure 3.5 suggests how the internal working model may become increasingly complex. Bretherton (1985) points out that when these scripts are activated they are accompanied by an emotional component. It is possible that the more basic or lower level representations are more likely to evoke the emotional component of memories since they are more closely connected to the specific episodes or memories of actual events that take place. In therapeutic conversations there can be a tendency to stay at the higher order representations, which are more general semantic descriptions. We will see later that the adult attachment interview specifically attempts to capture these lower order episodic representations along with the semantic higher order ones.

This model, which is drawn from Epsteins' self-theory (1973, 1980), also bears a strong resemblance to Kelly's (1955) personal construct theory (PCT). For Kelly the self was similarly at the centre of a person's personal constructs system. He argued that each of us develops a unique, hierarchically organized system of constructs. The constructs system evolves and changes and moves towards ever-increasing elaboration in how we are able to anticipate and predict events. As mentioned earlier, a construct is similar to the concept of a schema or basic script in that it contains meanings, implications for action and an evaluative or emotive component, in other words, how I feel about the person, event or relationship. Likewise Kelly (1955) argued that, though continually changing, the construct system was also resistant to major, dramatic or over-rapid change, especially of the core constructs. Change at the higher order constructs usually involved beliefs which are central to the self and provoke anxiety and hostility if challenged. As mentioned earlier there are further similarities in that constructs are bipolar divisions of the world and this resembles Bretherton's (1985) point that the attachment schemas contain two ends of a relationship, for example, cared for – caring for others or neglected – neglecting others. It is possible that connections between PCT and internal working models may be a fruitful endeavour. PCT employs a number of very elegant assessment methods, for example the repertory grid which offers a very similar picture of the hierarchical organization of a person's constructs. It might be interesting to develop grids of a person's attachments system and compare this, for example, to data from attachment measures, such as the Strange Situation or the adult attachment interview. The output of a grid analysis offers a very similar hierarchically organized picture as the one above (Epstein 1980; Bretherton 1985; Catlin and Epstein 1992).

In Figure 3.5 it is possible to see that the child appears to have a different attachment representation for the mother and the father, possibly a secure attachment to the mother and an avoidant one with the father. Viewing the working model as hierarchical it is possible to see that a child can hold a coherent representation of both systems by employing some higher order constructions to make sense of the disparity between his parents (see Figure 3.6).

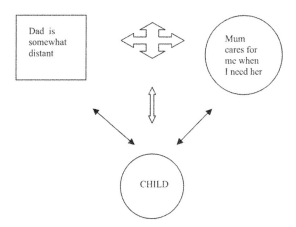

Figure 3.6 Different attachment patterns shown by parents towards a child

It is possible for the child to assimilate such a configuration into his internal working, especially if the parents, though different in their responses to the child, do not attack each other's approach or employ the child to get at each other. It is even possible for a child to hold a coherent working model if the parents separate:

> Mum and dad are not married any longer and though they do not like each other anymore they still each like me:
>
> 1 They are still each good *parents* to me
> 2 Both love me though they do not love each other

If marital conflict disrupts the parenting roles then it becomes more difficult for children to distinguish between the roles and confusion exists in the family dynamics.

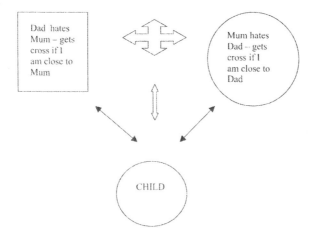

Figure 3.7 The child caught up in parental conflicts – attachment triangulation

The child's confusion can be seen then as an accurate representation of the family confusion. He or she may appropriately conclude that it is impossible to maintain positive emotional connections with both parents. The child therefore has difficulty in constructing coherence in terms of the relationship with each parent and any over-arching schema to help resolve the incongruities. A child in this situation is faced with a difficult task in developing a coherent working model. Instead, he or she may adopt a number of possible solutions:

1 Side with one parent
2 Intervene to resolve conflict
3 Withdraw altogether

Any of these solutions can help the working model to be clearer. The inconsistencies become fewer if the child completely rejects one parent, or both. Alternatively, the second option gives the child a higher order self schema of 'my role is to resolve their conflict'. However, all of these solutions, very well known to family therapists, result in the child losing important attachment relationships or becoming a carer and providing rather receiving attachment security.

Inconsistency and incongruity

As we have seen, such a hierarchical model of the internal working model helps to describe the patterns of schemas or beliefs that the child forms. But there is a need to discuss the problems further of how the child develops a working model when there is inconsistency between the parents and/or in the behaviour of either or both the parents. The most typical example of inconsistency is shown by a parent with an anxious/ambivalent attachment style. In this situation the parent gives contradictory messages, which makes it hard for the child to have a consistent model of the parent or of themselves (see Figure 3.8).

I like you   I hate you
You are bad   You are good
I will comfort you   I won't comfort you

Figure 3.8 Contradictory messages from parent with anxious/ambivalent attachment style

Bowlby (1969) has suggested that in this situation the child may develop multiple models of the attachment figure. One representation the child holds may be that the parent is loving but at the same time a competing sensory memory may be that he or she has been frightening and unavailable (see Figure 3.9).

> When multiple models of a single figure are operative they are likely to differ in regard to their origin, their dominance and the extent to which the subject is aware of them. In a person suffering from emotional disturbance it is common to find that the model that has greatest influence on his perceptions and forecasts, and therefore on his feelings and behaviour, is one that developed during his early years and is constructed along fairly primitive lines, but one that the person may be relatively unaware of; while simultaneously there is operating within him a second, and perhaps radically incompatible, model that developed later, that is much more sophisticated, and

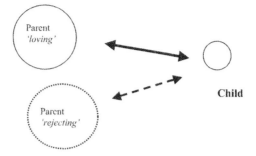

Figure 3.9 Incompatible models of a parent

that the person is more clearly aware of and that he may mistakenly assume to be dominant

(Bowlby 1973: 205)

A dominant view in attachment theory has been that such incompatibility is managed by a process of 'defensive exclusion' since, for example, the perceptions of the parent are so painfully incompatible, one of them is excluded or dissociated. Being out of awareness the assumptions are not subject to conscious reappraisal, discussion or testing to explore whether the perceptions are still true. As a result there is little opportunity for change and elaboration. Bowlby (1973) emphasized that problems arise when a child has to hold multiple models of her attachment figure and cannot find a way of resolving these into a coherent model.

Metacognition and reflective functioning

Main (1991) has suggested that an important feature of a child's development and a way of resolving contradictions and incongruity in or between his or her parents is to be able to develop meta-cognitions. These are in essence 'thoughts about thoughts'. In relation to conflictual family situations between parents or where the child experiences the parents as inconsistent, he or she may be able to resolve this by recognizing that he or she has mixed feelings and that these result from the contradictory way the parents behave. The idea of meta-cognition also connects with the systemic concept of meta-communication (Watzlawick et al. 1967) which is concerned with the importance of communication about communication to clarify misunderstandings or confusions. As we saw in the previous chapter, attachments can be seen as communicational processes and meta-cognition is an ability that may be fostered in a child through conversations which encourage reflection on what is communicated and what is not clear.

Importantly, Main (1991) traces the development of meta-communicational abilities to core mental development for the child and how this may be impeded by the nature of the attachment context. She argues that the skill of meta-cognition is linked to the basic ability of the child to separate 'reality' from 'appearance'. Put simply, this is the recognition that there is a real world 'out there' of objects, events, people and relationships. However, this world can be perceived in different ways by different people and one's view and understanding of it can change. It is suggested that children below 4 years of age tend not to be able yet to understand this and so are not able to question their own or their attachments figures' views. Piaget (1955) also described this in terms of young children's views of their parents as being omnipotent and all-knowing. Further, it is suggested that young children have difficulty with 'dual-coding', that something can also be seen in two different ways, for example that mother can be both 'nice', *and* also 'mean'. Main (1991) suggests that older children are therefore less vulnerable to difficult attachment experiences because they are able to form meta-cognitions. For example, parents saying, 'You are a bad child,' is more easily dealt with by an older child who is able to reason, 'I *may* be a bad person because Mum seems to think so, but, on the other hand, she has been wrong about other things, she is not always right'. For a younger child it is harder to resist the parents' perception. Moreover, a young child may be in a particularly vulnerable situation with a parent who is highly unpredictable and incongruous – as in the case of parents who are anxious/ambivalent or display a mixture of patterns (A/C or disorganized).

Particularly problematic may be situations where the parents engage in powerful distortions or deceptions regarding experience. In a study by Cain and Fast (1972) of children who had lost a parent due to suicide it was found that a quarter of the children had been subjected to pressure from the remaining parent to believe that they had been mistaken in what they had seen or heard. In one case a girl discovered her father's body hanging in a closet but was told later that he had died in a road accident. Main (1991) links such findings to the important question of children's ability to mark the source of information in their lives. Children under 3 years of age are less able to do this and are not easily able to tell if their memory of an event comes from their own memory or from what was told to them by a parent. Because older children are more aware of the source of the information and place greater value in what they themselves have experienced they are less prone to develop contradictory multi-models. This cognitive developmental perspective is important because it adds to explanations which stress mental suffering as the key explanation for why we hold multiple models and do not process or resolve the contradictions between them.

Fonagy et al. (1991a, 1996) has similarly emphasized that a central feature of the child's internal working model is the ability to engage in meta-cognition. He offers a broader concept which includes the ability to think about others' internal thoughts and feelings and that this is the fundamental ingredient of attachment processes. As does Main (1991), he suggests that it is the mother's ability to reflect on the child's internal state that is central: 'A child may be said to be in a secure relation to a caregiver to the extent that, on the basis of his or her experience, he or she can make an assumption that his or her mental state will be appropriately reflected on and responded to accurately' (Fonagy et al. 1991a: 215).

The parent's ability to be reflective is in turn acquired through her own childhood experience with her parents and it is argued that this 'reflective ability' is the core feature of the transmission of attachment patterns across the generations. The parents transmit to the child a sense of whether it is safe to engage in an exploration of people's feelings, intentions and beliefs. Fonagy et al. (1991a) have demonstrated a close link between reflective functioning and attachment patterns by developing a measure of reflective ability in parents (see AAI later) and the attachment style classification of their infants in the Strange Situation:

> We believe that cross-generational prediction is possible because attachment security in infancy is based on parental sensitivity to, and understanding of, the infant's mental world. The parent's capacity to understand the infant is rooted in the construction of coherent mental representations based on the parent's own attachment history
>
> (Fonagy et al. 1991a: 215)

This is also linked to Bion's (1962) concept of 'containment'. In understanding the child the mother is seen as both understanding what has caused the child to be distressed and also what the distress feels like. However, in addition the mother is seen as communicating that she does not feel overwhelmed by it herself. Fonagy et al. (1996) suggest that mothers who themselves have a dismissing pattern are likely to be able to transmit coping but not an understanding of what the child is feeling. Conversely, the preoccupied parents may be able to communicate that they understand the feeling, but are less able to communicate a sense of coping. West (1997) suggests that reflective functioning is biologically based and will develop naturally in humans unless impeded. This connects with the work on theory of mind (Baron-Cohen et al. 1993), which argues that to be able to understand others as having minds, thoughts, intentions, perceptions and to recognize that these can be different from our own is a fundamental ability and this ability is only absent where a person has severe problems such as autism. In fact, even the higher mammals possess the ability to some extent. It can be seen in their abilities to engage in simple forms of play, pretending and even deception (Bateson 1972; Baron-Cohen et al. 1993).

Reflective functioning and meta-cognition abilities are central to our ability to change. An important phenomenon is that some people, despite extremely adverse childhood experiences, appear to be able to create coherent internal working models. This suggests that reflective ability is available as a potential resource to help us to do this, though at the same time it may be impeded in various ways. It is also suggested (as will be discussed in Chapter 4) that the utilization and promotion of meta-cognition is a core feature of most forms of psychotherapy.

In summary, Fonagy et al. (1991a) argue that reflective functioning involves us in a variety of sophisticated mental activities. These include being able to reflect on our own thoughts, see contradictions in our views, contemplate alternative views, recognize from where our beliefs and memories arise, hold the view that it is possible to see things in different ways, recognize that we may have become stuck in a particular way of thinking, recognize the consequences of our thinking in particular ways, and recognize how we may be influenced by other's opinions. Some of the most severe psychological disorders appear to be linked to the breakdown of these abilities. For example, personality disorders appear to include a deficit in reflective functioning and this is seen to result from relationships in childhood where the child experiences negative and possibly abusive behaviour from a parent. This means the child is punished for showing attachment behaviours and any attempts to reflect on this punishment may also be further punished. At the same time the child may inhibit his or her attempts to be reflective and think about why the parent may be acting in this way, since the conclusion (she hates me, cannot be trusted, is dangerous, etc.) may be negative and produce further anxiety. A solution is to block these thoughts and not to engage in reflective processes regarding the parent. It has been suggested that this leads to a 'disorganized' attachment style (Fonagy et al. 1991a; Main 1991) but it might instead be possible to see this as organized and appropriate given the dysfunctional nature of the context the child is in (Crittenden 1997).

Attachment narratives

I have taken some time to review internal working models and how these can be seen as hierarchically organized schemas or systems of meanings. Added to this has been the important idea of meta-cognition and reflective functioning. The idea was also discussed that these can be seen as scripts which in effect are generalizations, based upon repeated observations of interactions. Stern (1985) has called these 'Representations of Interactions that have become Generalised' (RIGs) and Schank and Abelson (1977) have also described that our early understanding is built up from simple scripts. Byng-Hall (1995) has developed these ideas extensively by considering attachment and family life in terms of a broader and more complex view of scripts. This idea is similar to Goffman's (1959) ideas of human interaction as analogous to drama, with the idea of different scripts that we can play, people as actors and authorship of scripts. Byng-Hall's (1995) discussion of scripts connects with the idea of attachment narratives as stories that we come to hold about, and which come to shape, our experiences. In this section I want to discuss the relationship between attachment experiences in families and the development of the child's narratives. In addition I will discuss the idea of attachment experiences as held in different types of memory: visual, semantic, episodic and procedural (Crittenden 1997). Narratives can be seen to weave together these various components of our experiences: 'A narrative is composed of a unique sequence of events, mental states, happenings involving human beings as characters or actors ... Their meaning is given by their place in the overall configuration of the sequence as a whole ... its plot' (Bruner 1990: 44).

Representational systems

Crittenden (1995) suggests that it is important to distinguish between the representational systems that are being used when we talk about our attachment experiences. In the quote from Bruner above we can see that his idea of narrative contains the idea of different types of representations and importantly how these are organized into an overall pattern. Bowlby (1969) has suggested that the child develops multiple, incompatible models when faced with incongruous or traumatic events in his or her life. Especially problematic are situations where the child's experiences are invalidated and he or she is coerced into accepting a version of events which contradicts his or her own. Main (1991) originally distinguished between two primary systems: semantic and episodic memory. Drawing on contemporary cognitive psychology (Tulving 1972, 1983) a number of writers have extended this, especially Crittenden (1995, 2004) who discusses six main types of memory systems:

1   *Procedural memory*: These tend to be preconscious schemas involving the ordering of events and behaviours into sequences. An ordinary example might be driving behaviour whereby we are able to engage in the skills of driving without necessarily being aware, unless something unusual or unpredictable happens. Other examples include various skilled activities and musical performance where we can play a sequence without consciously being aware of what we are doing. A nice illustration of the temporal or procedural nature of such memory is that we often have to return to the start of a sequence in order to be able

to carry it out since the parts are connected in our memory as a chain of actions. In families this can be seen as interactional patterns, for example mealtimes and bedtimes routines as well as characteristic patterns of conflict.

2 *Imaged (sensory) memory*: This consists of memories involving visual images, smells, touch, sound and taste. These are associated with feelings and tend to remain in place through connection with dangerous (threatening) situations or exciting (for example, sexual) scenarios. The memories are seen as eliciting rapid identification or reminders of dangerous or exciting situations. People often describe how smells can trigger very powerful feelings.

3 *Semantic memory*: This is a linguistic and abstract form of memory consisting of verbal statements of how things are and causal explanations for them. It consists of statements in the form of 'if – then' sequences which can include information about feelings but at an abstract level ('if Dad is silent it's best to leave him alone'). These memories develop initially from what the child is told by the parent since initially children do not have the verbal skills to remember events in linguistic terms – they learn to do so from what their parents say. These memories start to be constructed towards the end of the second year of a child's life and at first the child may have difficulty differentiating his or her own from the parents' memories. Looking back at their childhoods people may comment that they are not sure if a memory is their own or something they have been told by a parent.

4 *Episodic memory*: This is a more complex form of memory involving a mental replay of events. It requires an integration of cognition and feelings and this includes weaving together sensory memories from various senses: sight, touch and smell. In order to engage in this we draw on information from various parts of the brain and weave these together in a coherent way. This type of memory is central to the ability to develop stories or narratives and tends not to emerge until the third or fourth year of life. As with semantic memory the child learns to do this in conjunction with adults and it is a co-constructional process. This biases the memories towards the parents' perspective in terms of both the content of the memories and how they are organized. The memories tend to focus on significant or important events and retention of these is important to help us recognize similar dangers in the future and in turn this can help a child to mentally construct alternative and self-protective

strategies. This might commonly be called 'learning from experience'. However, a danger can be that as we attempt to recall the events similar powerful feelings are evoked, and a similar response that was evoked originally, for example avoidance of the issues, pretending we don't care and so on, is repeated.

5   *Connotative language*: This is concerned with language that carries an emotional component. It is language which is rich in metaphor, analogy, visual connections and has the power to generate strong feelings in the listener. It is typically described as lively language; strong language in terms of swearing can also contain these features but it is the timing and presence not simply the presence of swearing, which can become repetitive and lose its power to evoke feeling if used predictably. Connotative language runs alongside the semantic memory as the 'verbalized form of imaged memory' system.

6   *Working memory*: This is seen to be the processing memory system that performs comparative and integrative functions. It is the 'live, on-line process of integration'. It is suggested that processing in the cortical area of the brain occurs in two parts. The first is a process whereby information from the various memory systems is held and compared with distracting information filtered out. The second process involves making connections with other information held to forge meanings and new connections. The process therefore involves the ability to recognize discrepancies between the information in the different memory systems and to generate solutions or plans of actions. Such analysis and integration takes time and this is difficult in dangerous circumstances when there is a need to act promptly.

Connecting with the discussion earlier of the hierarchical organization of the working models, the semantic memories are essentially higher level linguistic generalizations (for example, 'I had a supportive relationship with my mother'). Episodic memories on the other hand are specific instances of events with a mental replay of what happened and at the bottom level are sensory and procedural memories.

In short the development of narrative skills requires the child to develop abilities in integrating these various representational memories. The discussion earlier of the parents' role in facilitating the development of reflective skills is consistent with a burgeoning body of research on children's developments of 'narrative skills'. This research (Baerger and McAdams 1999; Habermas and Bluck 2000) indicates that the ability to author our lives into a coherent story is a highly complex 'skill'. Initially it seems that stories of young children around the age of 7 are relatively concrete, immediate and episodic. Their narratives do not span extended periods of time. Initially they hold relatively simple and concrete explanations for why people act in certain ways (Piaget 1955). When asked to talk about themselves, they tend to refer to immediate events, today or yesterday, to relate the concrete aspects of what happened, talk in terms of physical features of the participants and perhaps describe peoples' actions in terms of simple traits such as 'nice' or 'horrible' or 'very clever' (Habermas and Bluck 2000). This does not mean that they do not understand more about themselves and others than this, but that they may not yet have the language skills to express all of what they understand (Donaldson 1978). It seems that the ability to develop sophisticated narratives starts around adolescence (Habermas and Bluck 2000). Much of the work exploring narrative development has focused on the concept of *coherence* in narratives. This is seen to involve a number of components: setting the story in context, causal connections between events, an evaluation of events and a sense of purpose or a point to their lives. This also needs to make reference to culturally shared ideas of normative development of people's lives, transitional markers and expectations. For example, in adolescence there are culturally shared expectations of increasing independence, decision-making about careers and education, and sexual activity. The connecting of events requires an ability to think about other people's intentions and internal states and an ability to stand outside our stories and reflect on inconsistencies, gaps and details.

Language development is linked to the neurological development of the brain. Increasingly more sophisticated operations become possible as the complexity of the neuronal connections increases. However, the development of language abilities is a complex interplay between nature and nurture. The biological and the interpersonal development are interwoven and each facilitates the other. An important basis or 'scaffolding' for development of narrative skills arises out of the nature of the child's conversations with their parents. This requires parents to engage in conversations with their children to help teach them how to make sense of their lives, to connect events over time and to be able to weave together a thread of events being linked in a causal way. As a simple example, a study by McCabe and Peterson (1991) revealed that mothers' narrative styles could shape their young children's abilities to link events causally over time, as well as the level of detail and elaboration in their narratives. When assessed at 27 months, two infants had very similar abilities. Their two mothers had different styles in how they spoke to their infants, one emphasizing details in stories and the other causal connections. Eighteen months later the infants showed concomitantly striking differences in the way they told stories about things that had happened to them, the differences between them matching their mothers' styles.

Assessments of attachment narratives: story stems and the adult attachment interview (AAI)

Separation anxiety test: story stems

Much of the attachment research has been based on observational studies of children, originally in the home situation but increasingly in the Strange Situation protocol. However, increasingly interest has been directed (Oppenheim and Waters 1985) at how children start to form narratives of their early experiences and an interesting method that has been developed is the separation anxiety test (SAT). In this children, for example 6-year-olds, are asked to respond to six pictures showing a child of the same age and sex as themselves in various situations depicting separations. These vary in intensity from mild (being tucked up in bed) to extreme (parents going away for two weeks). The children are prompted to talk about what the depicted child might feel and why, and what he or she might do. They are also asked what they might do in a similar situation. Studies such as these repeatedly show that the children differ in the content and the organization of the stories that they are able to produce. For example, children who had years earlier been classified as secure in infancy were able to state that the child in the picture might feel sad or worried, but that the relationship with the parents was warm, the child was seen as valuable and help would be given when it was needed. By contrast, children who had been classified as insecure were able to say that the child was sad, but they had less positive views of the child and less faith that the parents would be available to help them. Often they were silent regarding what might happen to the child. The children differed in the nature or coherence of their stories, the insecure children being less able to be open and to offer details of what they felt, why they felt as they did and how the story might end. In addition they were less able to connect these with how the child in the story might feel and how they themselves would feel (Main et al. 1985). In effect their stories were less coherent in terms of explanations for how and why people were acting as they were and also in terms of consistency between their own and others' feelings.

Importantly, it was also observed that the way that the parents communicated with the children differed:

> The conversational discourse patterns of these six year olds paralleled their Strange Situation classification in infancy. Dyads in which the child had been classified as secure were fluent, discussing a wide range of topics. Those in which the classification had been avoidant were restricted in discourse, emphasising impersonal topics, showing little elaboration, and asking rhetorical questions. Dyads, including a

child who had been judged disorganised, were dysfluent and had many false starts

(Oppenheim and Waters 1985: 197)

Adult Attachment Interview (AAI)

This is a structured research interview developed by George et al. (1985) for use with adults, which typically means people over 18 though it is possible to employ a modified version with younger people. It normally takes about an hour to one and a half hours. It invites the interviewee to discuss their memories of their childhood experiences and in particular their patterns of attachments to the significant figures in their family. It has become one of the key procedures for assessing adults' attachment patterns and has reported validity with other measures, for example the attachment patterns shown by expectant mothers on the AAI were predictive of the attachment patterns that their children showed with them two years later in the Strange Situation (Fonagy et al. 1991a). The intention of the interview is to examine not only the content but the organization of the narratives that people present in the interview. A specific focus is on the level of consistency between their semantic and episodic memories. The interview consists of the following sections/questions:

BOX. 3.1   The adult attachment interview

General integrative questions
  1   Family context: Orient me to your family when you were a child
  2   Nature of relationships – attachment figures: Who were you closest to etc.?

Exploring semantic and episodic memory: for mother and father
  3   Attachment perceptions and memories: 5 adjectives/phrases

Exploring episodic memory further
  4   Comfort – danger threat distress: What did you do when you were upset, hurt

Difficult experiences/trauma
  5   Loss and separation
  6   Abuse, abandonment

Integrative questions
  7   Why do you think your parents behaved as they did?
  8   What have you learnt from the experiences? What effect has it had on your personality? What have you learnt about being a parent to your own children?

The AAI is intended to be live since the interview is seen as a communicative act, and the process of telling one's story to another human being is fundamental to eliciting the characteristic attachment patterns. This is consistent with a discursive perspective and the process of the interview is important, for example the strategies the interviewee employs to persuade, convince, deceive or involve the interviewer is relevant to the analysis. Crittenden (1997) explains that the AAI consists of four components. First, the interview is designed to assess different memory systems, especially semantic and episodic, and how the person is able to integrate these to offer coherent accounts. The integrative questions also invite them to engage in meta-cognition or reflective functioning to identify and comment on incongruities as they speak and to notice their own errors, distortions or omissions.

Second, the interviews are transcribed and subject to a form of structured discourse analysis. This focuses on the overall coherence of the accounts given, especially the coherence between the semantic and episodic memories. It also looks for patterns in the nature of the interview, for example the extent to which the discourse is overly semantic and lacking reference to feeling. Also of interest in the discursive analysis are the ability or difficulties in accessing memories, the extent to which there are confusions about the order and causes of events and identification of points where the speech becomes dysfluent and rambling. Consistent with discourse analysis the intention is to explore how the person tries to present, explain and justify their actions. Specifically, this includes a focus on the organization of the accounts not just the content – an attempt to consider what might be happening in terms of unconscious processes. Clues to this are seen to reside, for example, in how the person's speech alters when difficult or painful topics are approached. This can involve hesitations, changes of topic, non-verbal cues such as laughter, intrusion of vivid imagery, confusions of past and present location of events. Crittenden (1997) adds that the analysis should be expanded to focus on where it appears that information has been discarded, is erroneous, distorted or falsified.

The third component of the AAI is to synthesize the discourse analysis and attempt to classify the accounts. A considerable body of research exists to indicate that the transcripts can be reliably classified. These were originally classified as: secure, dismissing and preoccupied (Main and Goldwyn 1991). These classifications show broadly the same proportions as the classifications of the Strange Situation and are seen as representing the same attachment patterns. The classifications were subsequently increased to include a disorganized classification. There is considerable debate about whether this classification is helpful since it clusters together a whole range of clinical conditions. Furthermore, it assumes that the patterns are disorganized rather than functional and organized adaptations to dysfunctional and abusive social contexts (Crittenden 1997). Illustrative examples are offered in the next section.

Finally, the AAI was initially based on a theoretical position that views attachments as relatively permanent and enduring. There are some debates regarding this, for example a meta-analysis study by Van Ijzedoom (1995) is interpreted by Crittenden (1997) as showing that 'only 22% of the variance' was accounted for in parents (AAI) and their child classifications. In contrast Fonagy et al. (1996: 71) interpret this same summary as accounting for 'approximately one quarter of the variance . . . The association of the AAI and Strange Situation is 70 to 80 percent'! Probably, a reasonable conclusion is that continuity has been established and the parents' AAI is a powerful predictor of the child's attachment security. But, also that attachment representations are changing and the parents' AAI alone does not determine the child's patterns.

Content and organization of narratives

The following examples illustrate some key features of the classifications and the discourse markers employed.

Discourse markers: Dismissing narratives

The overall organization of these narratives centres on a shut down of episodic memories and an omission of feeling so that at times the accounts seem very dry and formal. The dominant strategy is to use semantic descriptions, sometimes in a very logical way, to avoid potentially painful memories of rejection. At the extremes the strategies can include examples of descriptions of caring for the parents when asked for accounts of being cared for, of memories from the parents' perspective and exoneration of parents even for serious neglect or abuse. Integration may be sparse with perhaps formal and theoretical statements about how events would or should have influenced the person rather than any evidence of personal changes.

A summary of the discourse markers in 'dismissing' narratives is:

- Omission of self from sentences about self;
- Use of distancing pronouns instead of personal pronouns;
- Omission of all people from statement;
- Minimizing of negative experiences;
- Nominalization of affect;
- Distancing phrases, cut-off phrases;
- Telegraphic speech, lack of details;
- Stilted, literary style of speech;
- Normalization of vulnerable self;

- Hypothetical phrasing;
- If–then, when–then contingencies;
- Strong denial of negative feelings.

The following quote is an example from an AAI transcript chosen to illustrate some of these key features of a dismissing narrative (Crittenden 2004):

Mark:	[Describing early relationship with his parents] There were close relations, very good relations. I suppose in my early years, my mother naturally featured more as my principal carer and provider of meals. Undoubtedly, it is to her that I went to on falling over and crying. I always remember both of them being there and supportive. I really have no reservations or major criticism at all about them as parents in the early years. My father, I suppose, became more influential as I grew older. But I think each had a very marked influence upon my life and almost entirely for the better. And I really can't record any negative aspects of that relationship, although, of course, there were many, the usual adolescent conflicts.
Mark:	[Describing comfort] I think tears were very frequent, but I probably ran to my mother, but I am guessing but I cannot remember. I remember cutting my hand badly on a shard of glass and screaming my head off and possibly running back home.
Int:	Running back home to your mom?
Mark:	Possibly, I can't remember

Discourse markers: Preoccupied narratives

These transcripts are often confusing and difficult to follow. There is often a lot of information about feelings and use of imagery but the information from different memory systems is often contradictory, for example, episodes or images that contradict the semantic description. There can be confusion in time and causes of events and between past and present so that it may be difficult to determine if the person is speaking about the past or the present. There can be examples of reflection but again this may be confusing or contradictory, or the content of it rather banal. At the extreme, interviews show oscillation between hostility and helplessness and also distortions and deception of self and others. At the most extreme the speakers adopt an extremely paranoid view of the world as being dangerous and menacing. To summarize, the features of these narratives are:

- Confusion of person;
- Confusion of time (oscillating between past and present);
- Confusing manner of speech;
- Vagueness of meaning through meaningless or qualifying phrases;
- Intrusion of irrelevant detail;
- Episodes told in the form of a dialogue;
- Passive semantic thought – does not come to a conclusion/point;
- Stream of consciousness flow of speech, without focused direction.

Illustrating this type of narrative are the following dialogues (from Crittenden 2004):

Int:	So you said 'secure but insecure' What are your memories of that?
Carol:	We were having this play for Christmas, um ... and um, I had practice that night, and for some reason I got Mom really upset. We were, um my sister and I were supposed to clean the kitchen up, and we emptied out the dishwasher, and we just threw the pots and pans underneath. We didn't stack them or anything and she went up later that night to open the cupboard and all the pots and pans came falling out, and she was really upset, she got really mad at us ... Well, she came out and she says, 'Alright, I've had it with you guys. I don't want to be your mother anymore,' and I was really upset. I cried for three days and she like ran in her room. Then she came back out and she goes, 'From now on you can call me Mrs Smith'

Lillian:	[Describing early relationship with her parents] As a little girl, I remember ... I think, hum ... I have always ... there has been always a real closeness between the two of us, hum ... because we were really similar, very similar, I just ... I feel for her all the time and I think she is the same, we are both very sensitive ... and I think ... maybe when I was small, when I was little, hum we spent a lot of time together, my mum didn't work she was always there for me, hum ... but I came to 12 years old and onwards that's when we started arguing ... constantly, and hum, yes but I feel an extreme closeness for her, I feel a lot for her, but, hum, its very turbulent and rocky, hum I have been trying, hum sort of think, about our relationship more lately, and, its not

> that, I don't know ... I think its because we are very similar, hum ... that ... it creates ... problems, may be something ...
>
> Int: When you were upset as a child what did you do?
>
> Lillian: I don't know, I can't remember, I used to run away apparently, hum ... So it used to get quite bad, so I would have a tantrum, and I still have tantrums, yes I still do it, but [laugh] ... yes, I used to throw things, you know like a psychic child, but that's all I can remember ... remember once being, I used to run away but I always came back, run away through the back garden because I was very tiny and it was a small hole in the fence where the cats used to go out and I went through there ...
>
> Int: Do you remember how old you were?
>
> Lillian: Yes, and my expedition always ended up somewhere [laugh]
>
> Int: So, how old were you?
>
> Lillian: Yes, I was probably about 3 or so, and I remember once I rolled and rolled and could not stop because I was so tiny and it was very windy and I ended up at the bottom of the hill, that was one of my expeditions out, running away angry.

Discourse markers: Secure

These accounts show good coherence between memory systems, ability to recall positive and negative experiences, ability to reflect on the experiences and evidence of integration of events. The person will often also show evidence of meta-cognition throughout the interview, for example taking account of whether they have explained something clearly enough to the interviewer – taking their perspective into account. Features of this narrative style are:

- Dysfluencies of speech, such as stutters, false starts, etc. but very few dysfluencies that distort information;
- Spontaneous recognition of inconsistencies or new thoughts;
- Evidence of meta-cognition.

The following extract illustrates this narrative style (from Crittenden 2004):

> Int: I would like you to describe the relationship with your parents when you were a child.
>
> Janet: As early as I can remember, I didn't have a very good relationship with my mother, I always had a feeling of – I was embarrassed, I was ashamed. I had a bowel problem. They told Mum I was dead when I was about three months old

and so they did Xrays and it wasn't until years later that they realized that it had done damage to my bowel. It was deformed. No one realized and they thought that I was a lazy little girl or something when I couldn't control my bowels and I'd come in from outside playing and I would have pood my pants and she thought I was too lazy to come in. It was still like that when I went to school. School was very traumatic. I grew up one of those children who hated kids. I hated other children. I loved animals but I hated kids. 'Janet, Janet the dirty old watermelon' was what I got. I'm laughing now but it wasn't funny then. Mum used to wash me in the trough and things like that. Perhaps I could understand now but I couldn't then. I think now, well dad worked away from home a lot ... He had his own business. He was up North a lot. She was mother and father to us three girls and the pressure was on her. She was only 33 or something. She would have got frustrated especially when there was nothing wrong physically with me. She used to say, 'Why do you do it?' and I used to say 'I can't help it. I can't help it'. She thought I was lazy. Dad I always had a good relationship with. He was my idol. I was one of those kids who was going to marry me dad.

Int: Changes in your relationship with your parents: what has happened over the years with Mum?

Janet: Well, in my early 20s all this sort of came back to me. I worked in a psychiatric hospital too – that made a lot of difference. I saw a lot of different people from different families and what had happened to them – most much, much worse than mine. Mine was nothing compared to these people. Just trying to understand where she was coming from. Was this woman as bad as I thought she was or as I have portrayed her? She can't be. She is my mother. I had to dig around a little and figure things out. My mother would say, 'We never had that' and I would say, 'Why not? How come?' and she never likes to talk about her past. Even now she won't. But I had to tell her how I felt and since then we have become closer. I still don't want to live with her. We have the real opposite personalities. I love her and she loves me but we couldn't live together but we are close.

In the extracts from Janet we can see that though the content of her story contains many painful and difficult memories yet she shows an ability to present these in a coherent form. Her semantic memories are congruent with the episodic detail. She describes a difficult relationship with her mother and offers convincing details of how and why this was difficult. This does not slip into idealizing or exonerating her mother as a dismissive narrative might. Neither does she become overly entangled emotionally as she tells her story. The narratives does not become fragmented, dysfluent, lacking clarity about time and place as it might if it was a preoccupied narrative. Also, she demonstrates that she has been able to integrate these experiences into a coherent story of how they have shaped her life, how she has transcended them and how she has resolved her relationship with her mother. Again, this is coherent and convincing in that she is still able to express both negative and positive feelings regarding her mother. Their relationship is not perfect but better than it was. She has also been able to empathize with her mother and develop an understanding of what life must have been like for her. Most of these features are clearly missing in the accounts from Mark, Carol and Lillian.

Pointer for therapy

The narrative assessments of attachment, through SAT and the AAI, allow an exploration not only of the content of attachment narratives but the way they are organized. In particular Main (1991) and Fonagy et al.'s (1991a) emphasis on the importance of meta-cognition as a central feature of the internal working model is incorporated into the two approaches. Fonagy et al. (1991a) have added an analysis of 'reflective functioning' as a further measure in the AAI. A number of studies have indicated that even when people have had extremely difficult childhood experiences they can still be successful in overcoming these if they are able to form coherent accounts of their experiences. Janet earlier is illustrative of such a process in having been able to transcend some very painful and humiliating childhood experiences. The importance of coherence has been described in various contexts. For example, Baerger and McAdams (1999) suggest that people's ability to form a coherent story is related to mental health even for people who have experienced some very difficult events. As we will see in the next chapter a critical concept for the narrative therapies emphasizes that the move away from self-destructive, oppressive, problem-saturated stories to coherent and integrated stories is central to therapeutic change.

Attachment theory has a considerable contribution to make here in a variety of ways. We know relatively little about how people move to coherent stories. Attachment theory, as in Janet's example earlier, suggests that the presence of one or more supportive attachment figures can assist the child to develop abilities, especially reflective functioning, so that they become able to integrate difficult experiences. It is also suggested that the process of therapy builds these abilities. In clinical populations it appears that because parents have been highly inconsistent, frightening and possibly abusive, the child's reflective abilities as a consequence may be inhibited. As discussed earlier if a child has not been encouraged to reflect, he or she may find it a dangerous prospect to reflect on his or her parents' intentions. Furthermore, the child's memory systems may be operating to distort information in various ways which makes it more difficult for reflective functioning to have any value. As Main (1991) clarifies there may also be developmental factors, for example, where younger children are more vulnerable to developing 'multiple models' or representations which are not integrated.

Secure base

One therapeutic consideration is first to offer some clarity and consistency along with a message of acceptance about the person. This is advocated by Byng-Hall (1995) in his idea of therapy as a secure base. In addition to this work, Crittenden (1997) suggests that it is helpful to understand the types of transformations of experiences in which clients are engaged in order to be able to orient our approach most helpfully:

> Each of the major schools of therapy seem particularly suited to effect transformations of a particular memory system. Behavioural therapies and family systems therapies focus on changing the contingencies on behaviours and making procedural models conscious, and thus available for examination and modification. Cognitive therapies focus on identifying and changing faulty semantic generalisations. Psychodynamic therapies focus attention on forgotten episodes and assist clients to work through feelings that were elicited long ago and left unresolved. Therapies that use visualisation and imagery address imaged memory in an effort to enable clients to free themselves from inappropriately preoccupying images and to facilitate use of comforting images to reduce anxiety. Finally, the various meditative therapies emphasise the need for distancing from active involvement in life tasks to achieve mental integration
> (Crittenden 1997: 55)

We will discuss these points further in the next chapter, especially in relation to the implications for systemic and narrative therapies.

4 Narrative systemic therapy: an attachment perspective

This chapter weaves together the threads developed in the previous chapters to consider how narrative systemic therapies are complemented by an attachment analysis. An overview of some of the core ideas and practices of narrative systemic therapy is outlined. These ideas are integrated with a systemic perspective on narrative therapy and in particular on co-constructional processes. Links are made to the discussion in the previous chapter about the nature of narratives and a consideration of how attachment processes are involved in the content and the organization of narratives. The discussion focuses on concepts of coherence of narratives and reflectivity, both of which are central concepts to attachment theory. In particular the chapter looks at the role that emotions and defences play in the construction of narratives and systemic processes in families. This sets the scene for the role of emotional processes in the context of therapy.

Narratives: definitions

In the previous chapter we looked at a range of interconnected concepts such as schemas, beliefs, scripts and narratives. Attachment theory has seen an important shift in emphasis to a conceptualization of attachment as being part of internal mental processes. The internal working model is seen to consist of a variety of processes that includes the idea of scripts and narratives. Two ways of exploring attachments – separation anxiety tests (story stems) and the AAI – have been developed to tap these narrative representations of attachments. The adult attachment interview in particular invites people to talk about their childhood attachment experiences. Though this is prompted by a number of specific questions, it can be seen that in their responses people in effect tell stories about their lives. The two terms *story* and *narrative* are closely connected. Typically a narrative is seen as one of the central ways that we organize and make sense of our experiences. A narrative contains the important idea of connecting or organizing our experiences over time. A narrative has a starting point, connected events over time which can be described as 'plot', a series of characters, a setting or context and some form of conclusion or point to the story:

stories ... establish the frames within which we become aware of self and others, within which we establish priorities, claim or disclaim duties or privileges, set the norms for appropriate and inappropriate behaviour, attribute meanings and order events in time ... Each given story is, in turn, embedded in a complex network of reciprocally influencing narratives. Individuals, families and larger collectives inhabit this system of multiple stories and organize their lives around making decisions in accordance with the dominant narratives

(Sluzki 1992: 219)

Narratives can be grand, as in autobiographical narratives – the story of our life or of a notable event in our life. Bruner (1990) has argued that narratives are perhaps the fundamental building block of human experience or the 'mind'. When we talk with others or have inner conversations these tend to be in the form of narratives or stories. He suggests that narratives importantly have the power not just to represent what has happened but also imaginary events. A narrative is evocative, it conveys feelings and captures not just the events that occurred but what they meant to the speaker and how he or she felt about the events (Bruner 1990). In talking about their problems family members may convey, through the description of the events and incidents, their sense of helplessness, frustration or shame. As we listen to a narrative it also can help us to connect personally to the events and to become involved in the unfolding story. For example:

If he was going to spank us, it was called a discussion and we had to go to his office for a discussion and he ... I remember I think I was only ever spanked by him on one occasion that I can remember. It was with a paddle and I was over his, uh over his knee and he, I remember him saying, explaining why he was going to do it – even at the time realising that he was trying to justify himself why he was gonna do it and I was in tears before I was spanked because it was such a, ugh, you know, agonising situation. At times he was quite crazy and jokey but he's – um – I remember him being quite serious and worried about things

(James, from Crittenden 1997: 64)

The power of the narrative not just to describe but to evoke powerful feelings and personal connections is illustrated above; we can imagine the situation and what it must have felt like for James as a young boy and make connections to situations where we were similarly frightened, confused or intimidated. As Crittenden (1997) has suggested, the narrative contains within it a depiction of affect through connotative language which captures sensory memories, images, metaphor, analogy and the pattern or 'poetry' of the language.

Narratives are also communications or communicative acts. The AAI and story stems, as we have discussed, involve the person communicating as they tell their story of their childhood attachment experiences. A narrative is therefore a performance and, as we have seen in the discussion of the AAI, we activate different memory systems and emotional processes in the act of talking and telling our stories. This can be seen not just as a process of telling but of performing, acting out or living our stories. In articulating our story we remember events and the emotions aroused in us can parallel the feelings that occurred at the time of the experiences we are describing. Furthermore, this is an interactional, communicational process in that as we tell our story to another human being we direct, shape, monitor and adjust the telling so that our listener can follow it and is connected to the story. A narrative approach stresses that each telling can become an interpersonal co-construction so that in the telling the story may be modified, and we may gain new insights as we tell the story. It is not simply, or predominantly, like turning on an audio-tape that faithfully produces the same story every time we press the 'on' button. Narrative therapies aim to encourage this constructive process but do not attempt to control it. Instead talk is in itself seen as constructive, gen-erative and changing. Narrative therapy attempts to harness and promote this natural process.

Content and organization of narratives: coherence

In the discussion of the AAI we have seen that the way people organize their stories about their childhood attachment experiences can be classified into particular overall styles. These styles involve various forms of transformations of experiences especially in the ways that emotional or cognitive experiences are either relegated or emphasized. An important aspect of the description of the accounts in the AAI is the extent to which these transforming processes render the stories coherent or incoherent. This idea of coherence has important connections to narrative therapies which emphasize that an ability to develop a coherent story about our lives is at the core of positive change. It is argued that even where people have experienced profoundly difficult, negative and even abusive experiences, these can be transcended if we are able to develop a coherent account of the experiences.

Before we look further at the notion of coherence we can look at the various ingredients of narratives. Various attempts have been made to offer outlines of narratives but an important distinction is drawn between the content and the organization of narratives. This connects with the discussion of the narrative attachment approaches in the previous chapter in terms of the explicit content of the narrative and how it is organized. In summary, narratives contain the following features:

> - *Organized over time*: A description of events and their meanings in a connected form. Like a story, a narrative usually has a beginning, a middle and an end. It serves to make sense of experiences for self and others and so is typically used to explain and justify actions.
> - *Selectivity*: Narratives not only depict but select some events, they shape perception and memory.
> - *Difference*: Narratives revolve around difference and contrast, for example between problem-saturated narrative and a problem-free narrative.
> - *Self*: A central feature of our narrative is the construction that we evolve about our self in relation to others: how we prefer to be seen vs. how we are seen.
> - *Dysjunction*: The larger the difference between preferred and actual narratives about the self, the greater the distress we experience.

Distinction can be made between narratives in a person's narrative system. For example, we can think of some narratives as 'core' in that they capture essential beliefs; we hold as important the narratives about values and ethics of family life and relationships. These are likely to be related to central aspects of self. Narratives can also be seen as changing and evolving or escalating. For example, narratives can polarize, for example, a story of who is 'good' vs. 'bad' becomes more extreme. Narratives can be seen as shared or as family paradigms in that they represent commonly held beliefs in a family, for example a belief that 'showing feelings is dangerous' (Reiss 1980; Procter 1981; Dallos 1991). Relating to the idea of narratives as shared it is also possible to regard them as offering positions in a dialectical process. Family members may agree on a dominant narrative that they have problems, but take different roles and see different potentials, for example, on who or what is the cause of the 'problem' and what will happen.

Coherence

Baerger and McAdams (1999) suggests that in any given culture there are ideas or rules about what constitutes a good, clear, coherent story. Alongside cultural variations researchers have paid attention to two ideas about structure. One is to focus on how a story offers a set of episodes which are linked in a temporal and causal sequence. The story starts with some setting or orientation, some initiating event which sets it into motion with some type of goal or aim and description of unfolding events with some point, or resolution, of the story. However, this offers a rather cognitive and structural view of narrative and coherence. Labov and Waletzky (1967) and Bruner (1990) emphasize that the emotional tone and development of narratives is a central feature – that stories exist to convey emotionally significant information. Stories that just conveyed the facts are bare and 'boring'. Instead, Labov and Waletzky (1967) argue that we invariably tell stories organized around emotional highpoints. A story, he argues, is organized around a series of dramatically ordered events which build up to an emotional pinnacle followed by some resolution that settles the emotional tone. In essence, he argues that a story is coherent in that it successfully 'conveys some emotionally significant information about the narrator on, or about what the events described therein mean to him or her' (Baerger and McAdams 1999: 72). Baerger and McAdams offer the following as a structure for coherence of a narrative (adapted from Baerger and McAdams 1999: 81):

> * *Orientation*: The narrative introduces the main characters and locates the story in a specific temporal, social and personal context. The narrative describes the habitual circumstances which serve as the parameters for the action of the story.
> * *Structure*: The narrative has a structure which includes the following: an initiating event, an internal response to this event (e.g., thought, feeling, plan), an action or attempt to do something about this (e.g., fix a crisis, carry out a plan, sort out feelings) and a consequence.
> * *Affect/emotion*: The narrative shows something about the storyteller and what the events mean to him or her and the story offers some evaluation or judgement about the events. The storyteller uses emotion to make the evaluative point, using explicit statements about their own and others' feelings to create an emotional tone to the story. The storyteller uses tension, drama, humour or pathos to communicate and emphasizes the evaluative point – the meaning of the story.
> * *Integration*: The narrative conveys information in an integrated way, especially in conveying the meaning of the experiences within the wider context of the person's life story. Discrepancies, inconsistencies and contradictions may be noted and resolved so that there is a unifying story. The story may employ complexity, ambiguity and differences to indicate conflict, suspense, insight and awareness or revelations. The narrative manages to reconcile these elements with one another.

It is important to note that this scheme of coherence is organized around the integration between emotional states and events. This is close to the emphasis in the AAI on the integration between information from episodic and semantic memory systems. It is also important to note that the emphasis on emotions is missing in much writing on narrative therapy. Arguably, all therapists deal with emotions as central to their work but the narrative therapists describe their work much more in structural and semantic terms. This point is emphasized later in this chapter in Coulehan et al.'s (1998) research, which indicates that emotional processes are central in narrative therapy.

Baerger and McAdams (1999) employed this structure of coherence in accounts to explore the relationship between coherence and psychological well-being. They asked 50 participants to complete a variety of standardized measures of psychological well-being. They were also asked to undertake a life story interview, giving a general portrayal of their life with some specific points of focus: a peak experience, a nadir experience, a turning point experience, a childhood scene, an adolescent scene, an adult scene and one other important memory that they could choose. Baerger and McAdams's findings were that it was possible to rate coherence using their scheme and that the rating corresponded closely to reported psychological well-being. Interestingly, coherence was not simply linked to positive or negative experiences. For example, participants who displayed indications of depression or other emotional problems were equally likely to be less coherent when describing positive or negative experiences:

> episodes related by the more depressed participants ... appeared to derive no meaning from their experiences. As a result, the stories they told seemed detached or alienated from the larger context of their lives. In contrast, the life episodes related by the more coherent participants not only strongly reflected the participants' overall life themes, but they also communicated ... a profound sense of the meaning the events had for [them]
>
> (Baerger and McAdams 1999: 93)

They concluded that their study was one of the first to support the view of narrative therapists that mental well-being is related to a well integrated and coherent life story. As we have seen in the previous chapters, the extent to which people are able to develop an integrated story about their lives is linked to the nature of the attachment system that they have experienced as children and also the attachment systems in place in the adult relationships.

Narratives and social constructionism

We will return to the question of the emotional content of narratives consistent with the communicational and interpersonal view of attachment and the development of attachment narratives. The narrative therapies are strongly influenced by social constructionism (Gergen and Davis 1985) which argues that our social world, unlike our physical world, is not a pre-given but is actively created. Social constructionism gives priority to language and argues that language contains the 'building blocks', the materials from which we construct our experiences (Foucault 1975; Gergen and Davis 1985). Like systemic theory and attachment theory, social constructionism sees interaction and communication as central and it is in the processes of conversation that meanings are mutually shaped. Rather than seen as essentially located within individuals, meanings are seen to be co-constructed so that with each conversation new meanings, interpretations and nuances are developed. Importantly, it is suggested that even in our private moments, our thinking features internalized conversations with others. As an example, I may rehearse conversations that I wish to have with people, or attempt to edit conversations that I have had in order to get my point across better, in other words, think of what I wish I had said. A central idea of social constructionism is that meanings are held in the form of discourses. These are constellations of beliefs or narratives.

Broadly, social constructionist approaches can be seen to have two main strands:

- *Top–down*: Experience as shaped by our internalization of dominant discourses (Hollway 1989; Gergen 1999). These might be ideas about what is thought to be 'normal' and acceptable in family life, how children should be disciplined and what counts as mental health. This also suggests that any society has a range of dominant ideas or ideologies which have power and influence at any particular time. Another powerful example is that the major global drug companies have the financial resources and influence to support medical models of various forms of psychological distress because it is in their interest to do so to promote sales of expensive psychiatric medications.
- *Bottom–up*: At the same time as recognizing these dominant influences from our shared culture, social constructionism also argues that meanings are shaped locally in everyday conversations. Dominant discourses exist, they are given meanings, within the uniqueness of the combinations of specific interactions and the participant's personal biographies. They are not objective entities but continually shifting waves of meanings.

Meanings are co-constructed but importantly that they are also seen to be contested and negotiated at both the local and the global level. In everyday conversations people are seen to argue over the meanings of their specific actions as well as over political and moral discourses, for example the nature of problems in a family and more generally the nature of mental illness in a given culture.

A central feature is that identity is seen to be fluid and shifting rather than stable and made up of static 'personality traits'. Beliefs, schemas, attitudes are seen as connected to particular contexts and relationships rather than inherently within the person (Potter and Wetherell 1987; Gergen 1999). This is consistent with an attachment perspective that views internal working models as created in relation to different relationships. This also offers a challenge to approaches, such as cognitive behavioural therapies which attempt to alter patterns of 'dysfunctional' beliefs. Social constructionism emphasizes context and interpersonal processes in creating joint actions. This connects with evidence from developmental psychology (Trevarthen 1980; Trevarthen and Aitken 2001) and attachment theory, which suggests that from birth babies are connected and synchronize with their mother's actions. From initially simple reflexes this extends to exchanges involving pleasure and comfort, and rapidly to preverbal games such as teasing, pretending and so on. Meanings are seen as mutually constructed. Development is seen to involve 'intersubjectivity' in that the emergence of joint action and joint construction of meaning is based on the ability of participants to develop understandings of each other's experience. This connects with 'theory of mind' and 'reflective functioning' discussed in the previous chapter where the child is able to view others as acting intentionally on the basis of their views, beliefs and explanations, and a recognition that these may contrast to his or her views.

Social constructionism also regards interaction as strategic. Language use is seen as pragmatic in that it is employed to achieve desired outcomes and, in particular, to present self in acceptable ways. There is a focus on 'rhetorical strategies' – the ways language is used to achieve certain ends, for example to persuade, accuse, justify, solicit sympathy or admiration, or seduce. A variety of linguistic strategies is seen to be employed to achieve these ends such as use of humour, presenting arguments *in extremis*, emphasizing one's honourable intention, use of metaphor and reference to stereotypes or shared images, metaphors and stories. Interactions are seen as inevitably involving negotiation and power, especially where people are seen as struggling over whose meanings will prevail (Haley 1987). These contests over meaning arouse and can escalate feelings such that the frustrations can spill over into actions and aggressions, 'to *make* the other see it my way'.

Narrative therapy

The narrative therapies take as their central aim the transformation of the stories that people hold about themselves and the important others in their lives:

> The goal of the therapist is to facilitate or promote ... change in specific stories ... Since stories are located in the shared realm of consensus, the therapist ... will attempt to generate a conversational environment that facilitates shifts of consensus; they will maintain a stance of openness about their intent, they will empathetically open themselves to the family's pains and struggles, they will maintain a stance of interest and curiosity about the family's ideas, they will favour an optimistic stance of positive connotation, and they will actively contribute to shaping the therapeutic conversation towards change in the collective story.
>
> (Sluzki 1992: 219)

White and Epston (1990) describe how pathologizing stories may come to dominate and restrict people's potential avenues of action. This oppression is fuelled by wider discourses or culturally shared beliefs, particularly in Western societies, that distressed states or experiences are a result of inherent personality flaws, organic deficits or biologically inherited tendencies. Family members and others may come to describe themselves and each other in terms of pathologizing and totalizing language as seen, for example, when people are referred to as 'anorexics' or 'bulimics' and these definitions are seen to constitute the totality of who they are. Such terms may become internalized and over time come to shape, and eventually consume, the whole of a person's identity to the point where aspects of their lives, other than that related to problems of, for example, food become marginalized. In families some of the processes whereby this occurs have been described as 'problem saturated' conversations (Anderson et al. 1986). If initial difficulties in a family lead to conversations which focus on their inadequacies, how they are failing, then there may be a progressive drift or a 'pathway to pathology' in which their talk gradually shifts exclusively to a concern with their problems. This eventually can lead to an exclusion of any talk which can recognize exceptions to the problems or the family's competencies (Eron and Lund 1993; O'Hanlon 1994; Dallos and Hamilton-Brown 2000).

Many narrative-informed therapists work with individuals and share fundamental premises with other individually oriented therapies, such as holding as central the connections between the person, their emotional experience and the therapist. Narrative-informed therapists take this premise further than some psychodynamically informed therapists by their reflexive stance, so that the client's lived experience is believed to be not only the client's story but the lived experience of the client and therapist working together. Narrative approaches emphasize that our beliefs and understandings are fundamentally structured into stories or narratives, which connect events, experiences, actions and feelings over time.

The writer, Salman Rushdie, uses a metaphor of a 'sea of stories' which nicely captures the idea that any given culture can be seen as holding a repertoire of shared stories. In Western cultures we all know the stories of Sleeping Beauty and the Prodigal Son. We connect with these stories and employ them in our conversations with others to capture and share ideas, such as our life as a struggle against adversity, deception, exploitation by others, or ideas of being outcast and resolving troubled relationships. In addition there are personal stories that develop within families. Narrative therapy emphasizes how these stories have a place in culture and transmit a continuity of ideas over time. In families they give a map to our experiences and relationships with each other. This feature of narratives as both personally and culturally shared prompts narrative therapists to reflect on how to weave together the personal, unique as well as culturally shaped aspects of experience.

For narrative therapists language is central and within language the phrases, metaphors and proverbs construct a continuity of ideas. In effect it is through language that a cultural evolution takes place. Narrative therapy is then centrally concerned with the stories that people hold about themselves and each other. In turn it seeks to reveal or discover with families how particular stories may be holding them in positions of distress. Of particular significance here are stories about deficit and essential personality characteristics. These also connect with medical models which feature stories of illness and abnormality. A core idea shaping narrative therapies is to expose these negative stories and explore how they are serving to maintain problems.

The therapeutic process: restorying and multiple descriptions

At the heart of narrative approaches is the idea that in altering our stories our experience of ourself and others can dramatically alter. Furthermore, it takes the view that it is not helpful to secure fundamental truths but to think of narratives as more or less helpful, freeing and enabling. White and Epston (1990) have summarized some of the key elements of a narrative approach to therapeutic practice, which, when used in combination, give the approach its distinctive narrative flavour:

1	Exploring relevant aspects of lived experience and developing varying perspectives on this;
2	Exploring the connectedness of events and relationships over time;
3	Exploring implicit meanings with exploratory conversation;
4	Identifying those influences which affect the 'ownership/ authorship' of stories and emphasizing the person as a participant in the story with some power to re-author it;

5 Identifying dominant and subjugated discourses in a person's accounts and the prevailing arrangements of privilege and power;
6 Using different 'languages' to describe experience and construct new stories;
7 Mapping the influence of the problem on a person's life and relationships;
8 Establishing conditions in which the subject of the story becomes the privileged author;
9 Externalizing the problem; and
10 Recognizing unique outcomes.

The means whereby this is achieved is a subtle process of communication and co-construction of new or altered stories. Change is often accompanied by a powerful emotional sense of release and freeing, not just for the family but also for the therapist. I can recall many experiences where what has signalled a significant turning point in therapy was my own ability to develop a different story about the problems. A two-way process can be seen to occur where the family provides information, fragments of narratives and ideas, and from the flux of their communications and from my questions and our shared attempts to make sense some new stories start to emerge. As I become able to communicate that I can genuinely see things differently it becomes possible to move towards a shared new and more hopeful story. Sluzki (1992: 220) also describes a similar process:

> In the course of the therapeutic conversation ... the therapist ... through questions and comments, favours certain kinds of trans-formations in the nature, in the telling of the stories, and/or in the relationship between stories ... alteration in the content of the story, as well as the way it is told, will trigger changes in plot, characters, setting, and theme ... these shifts in turn alter the storyteller's experience of the world ... and ... will affect the way problems are conceived, perceived, described, judged, and enacted

He goes on to describe therapy as involving a number of identifiable stages. Though the encounter is seen to be idiosyncratic, some overall 'blueprint' can be discerned:

- *Framing the encounter:* The initial conversations frame the encounter in terms of the therapeutic relationship. Defining some ideas about how the therapy and the therapist are viewed and issues of power – what the hopes and aims of the meetings are and expectations of the therapist. It also involves the nego-tiating and establishing of areas of collective agreement.

- *Eliciting and enacting the dominant stories*: This involves eliciting information about the nature and context of the problem or conflict – the dominant stories and their themes and structure.
- *Favouring alternative stories or relations between stories*: This involves encouraging new information or alternative views and noting and underlining exceptions that question the dominant stories.
- *Enhancing the new stories*: Once new stories or nuances start to emerge the therapist attempts to support, consolidate, bolster and build on these by validating them and encouraging further details to support them. Typically this involves a shift away from pathologizing, blaming, individualistic stories to ones that feature relationships and an awareness of how their experiences are connected to relational events, external changes and the ability to work collaboratively to transcend difficulties.
- *Anchoring the new stories*: This can involve attempts to anchor the new stories by suggesting and encouraging activities, such as tasks, celebrations and rituals that support the stories.

More specifically Sluzki (1992) suggests that the transformation processes involve shifts in a number of ways. These include transformations in:

- *Time*: When did the problems start? Did the bickering become more or less marked when you took your new job?
- *Contexts*: Where did the problems start? Where are they least/ most debilitating?
- *Causality*: In terms of 'punctuation', i.e., what led to what. For example, who started the arguments as opposed to a view of it as a reciprocal escalating process.
- *Interactions*: Explanations of causes as being inside persons, personal, essential qualities or relational.
- *Intentions/effects*: Views of people's intentions, especially ideas of negative, malicious and manipulative intentions, for example attentions seeking intentions or selfish gratification.
- *Values*: Related to intentions are deeper values, for example, what it means to be a 'good' mother or father, what are appropriate ways of acting sexually and so on.
- *Telling of the story*: This includes shifts in whether the person is telling the story as a passive victim of events, subject to others' actions on them, or as an active agent or author of the events in their life.

Narrative therapies tend not to be focused on techniques; however, they contain a number of orientations in terms of how some of these transformations may be encouraged.

Externalizing

This connects with Sluzki's idea of agency and telling of the story. Central to this is an attempt to separate the problem from the person. Rather than seeing the problem as some fundamental quality inherent in, or an essential part of, the person, it is portrayed instead as an externally driven, temporary, unwelcome and transient state that has entered into the person's life. Typically the problem has become a central part of the person's identity, a process which is exacerbated by diagnostic processes, for example, when a person is referred to, and comes to see themselves as an anorexic, a schizophrenic or as personality disordered.

People are encouraged to see the problems as external to them, to resist the problem and this process of its intrusion into their life by regarding it as external to them, something that has entered into their lives as an unwelcome visitor. In turn they are encouraged to see themselves as active agents and supported in considering ways that they can work together with the therapist to resist the problems and gather strength. Such an approach is pertinent to many problems, including eating disorders, to resist the powerful processes of 'body fascism' – the pressures on women to confirm to culturally valued ideas of beauty as involving slim youthfulness. Narrative therapies attempt to separate the problems from the person. The narrative process of externalizing the problems attempts to fragment this process by looking, for example, at how anorexia has come to dominate and terrorize life in a family. Externalizing of the problem also involves an exploration of potentially oppressive stories about the causes of anorexia. This can include a view that women with this problem are manipulative, that it is a form of control or that it is a covert attack or retaliation on their mothers. Such personal, or even family, stories are seen as pathologizing individuals and relationships and distracting attention from the wider social and cultural processes, for example of how anorexia is promoted by a culture which emphasizes the need to control women's bodies and places undue emphasis on women's appearance. This process also serves to shift the systemic context in such a way that other people, such as family members, are encouraged to assist the person to resist the problem rather than engaging in processes of blaming or mutual sense of failure.

This approach involves encouraging people to objectify and sometimes personify difficult problems. This way, the problem becomes external to the person and capable of being described, spoken to, talked about, and so on. Thus, if fixed or inherent qualities have been attributed to the person, those same qualities become more fluid and dynamic in this process. At the same time, family members trying to help solve the problem may have become dispirited by the apparent lack of success and have subjected themselves to a similar process of self-reinforcing negative attribution. The effects of this process can be heard when family members come to their first meeting. They are likely to describe themselves and their difficulties using a 'problem-saturated description' and this has becomes the 'dominant story of family life' (White and Epston 1990). Thus the process of externalization helps all family members separate themselves and their relationships from the problem, and opens up opportunities for them to begin to describe themselves and their efforts anew, using systemic processes of reframing and positive connotation.

Externalizing the problem has similar effects to that of Socratic questioning used by cognitive therapists, whereby some psychological distance is created in relation to a problem that felt overwhelming or overwhelmed a person's ability to think about it. Similarly gestalt therapists might personify some aspects of a person's problem. For example, a child who has recurrent stomach aches with no apparent organic cause and who is struggling to attend school might be asked to talk to his or her stomach ache, which might be named and 'invited' to sit in the adjacent chair. Such a procedure would be aimed at helping the child articulate the basis of his or her worries and concerns.

Unique outcomes

This approach is shared with the solution-focused approaches and essentially involves attempts to find exceptions to the dominant story of failure, hopelessness and inevitable deterioration. In part this can include a shift in time frames so that the person or family is asked to think about a time before the problem came into their lives and times when they were able to function adequately, or when they were able to master the problems. This invites people to search for exceptions and successes which, it is argued, have become subjugated stories, often out of everyday awareness or rarely discussed in family conversations. In part it encourages a shift in attention to details and experiences which validate a sense of failure to attention to events and actions which suggest success and competence. As the conversation shifts to explorations of competence, by a process of association, further details may be triggered leading to further recall of other instances. Where people experience great difficulty in identifying exceptions they may be invited to imagine or to think about hypothetical unique outcomes; what would it look like to be able not to feel oppressed by the problem, what would they be doing, what would others be doing, how would this feel and so on.

Dysjunctions: viewing – doing stories

A central aspect of narrative approaches is that our sense of identity consists of a set of stories or narratives about past events, current events and our potential futures. In addition a central division here is between our preferred or desired view of self and an actual or in some cases non-preferred or deviant view. This sense of preferred vs. non-preferred stories also connects to our socially shared world or reality. Eron and Lund's approach (1993) features an emphasis on exploring such dysjunctions and looks at these within a framework of 'punctuation' suggested by Watzlawick et al. (1974) and Bateson (1972). This suggests that a narrative punctuates or frames cycles of interaction which in effect have no beginning or end. However, each participant sees a story, often in terms of when events started, what the causes are and their own role, often as reacting to the events. This also connects with an approach called family construct psychology developed by Procter (1981) which offers a framework which regards actions and beliefs/narratives in terms of self-maintaining cycles. Eron and Lund (1993) speak instead of the preferred and non-preferred narratives that family members hold. The schisms or dysjunctions between our preferred and non-preferred stories is seen as central. For example, we may feel sad, angry, depressed or desperate when we feel there is a strong split between the two. As an example they describe how a story of depression evolved in a family where Al, the father, is recovering from having suffered a heart attack:

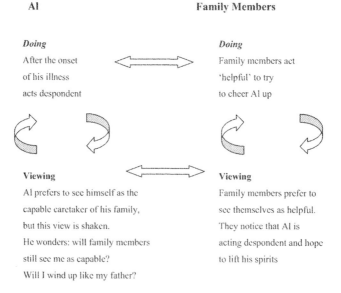

Al   **Family Members**

Doing   *Doing*
After the onset   Family members act
of his illness   'helpful' to try
acts despondent   to cheer Al up

Viewing   *Viewing*
Al prefers to see himself as the   Family members prefer to
capable caretaker of his family,   see themselves as helpful.
but this view is shaken.   They notice that Al is
He wonders: will family members   acting despondent and hope
still see me as capable?   to lift his spirits
Will I wind up like my father?

Figure 4.1 Narrative: viewing–doing cycles

They describe how such a cycle of narratives and the actions based on them can lead to an escalation of problems. As the cycle progresses Al comes to see himself as less and less capable and the family members come to see themselves as incapable. The family also come to see Al as ungrateful and he in turn comes to resent them and sees them as interfering and disrespectful. In this cycle we can see dominant culturally shared stories about what it is to be a man, father, children, family life, impacts of illness as well as the presence of transgenerational family stories. In Al's case there was a story that his father had in his later years become chronically depressed, alcoholic and a liability on his family. This spectre of dependency haunted Al and the family.

Eron and Lund's form of narrative therapy involves working with the family to consider both alternative stories and also experimenting with alternative ways of acting: attempted solutions. As an example, discussions take place about the differences between Al and his father, about times that Al had been competent and discussions of what he can still do and how his strength may be regained slowly. Also, the importance in convalescence of staying active and exercising is considered, so that the family works together to enable Al to do progressively more.

A question regarding narrative approaches relates to the potential differences in narrative processes and abilities. Attachment theory reveals that a variety of transformational and potentially distorting processes operate. Further, the approach privileges what is said, rather than the way in which it is said, and de-emphasizes the role of observation and the importance of non-verbal communication in therapy and in people's lives. There is a risk that the emphasis on authorship of one's own stories plays down the role of social, political and economic factors on people's lived experience, despite the recognition within the approach of the influence of power arrangements.

Reflecting processes and reflective practice

Tom Anderson (1987) has developed a version of narrative therapy which employs the idea of multiple narratives of descriptions. This consists of an open team discussion about a family, couples or even individual clients held openly in front of them. One variant in practice is for the supervising team to discuss their reflections of the therapy while the therapist and family members listen. The team's discussions are seen as helping and encouraging family members to consider alternative explanations, stories and attributions regarding their lives together. At times, the reflecting team may disagree and debate different possible ideas and explanations among themselves. This may allow different family members who hold opposing views to feel understood and perhaps enable them to move on to more constructive points of view. Importantly the reflecting team enables family members to hear and perhaps begin to internalize a different conversation rather than simply different explanations. By being able to internalize different conversations they are, in Bateson's (1972) terms, 'learning to learn', or being encouraged to become more creative. The therapy thereby becomes less concerned with content and less in danger of being marooned in attempts to offer families a 'better' view or story. The reflecting team offers a variety of narratives that invite a family to think in different ways but leaves them the choice of what might make a better fit. Apart from the content of the discussion they may experience a different process of conversation by, for example, hearing the team discussing potentially difficult and conflict-laden issues in a less emotional way. In a sense this can be viewed as a form of modelling but the process is less directive and more collaborative in its intent.

Change and emotions in narrative therapy

Sluzki (1992) and other therapists (for example, De Shazer 1982) argue that the new stories provided by these reflecting teams need to contain components from the family's own viewpoint or they will be rejected as too different and not related to the family's own experiences. Likewise, stories that are too similar will have little impact. What underlies this process of change are feelings. Coulehan et al. (1998), in a study of the process of narrative therapy, discovered that points of transformation were marked by important shifts in emotions. This study looked at a version of narrative therapy based on Sluzki's ideas of transformation of meaning as being central to the process. Work with eight families and eight trained family therapists was explored. The study explored transformations in terms of the therapist eliciting the old story and then working with the family to create a new story. This typically involved a transformation from a story which featured individual factors and blame to a new story focusing on interpersonal dynamics, exceptions and values. The therapy featured child-focused problems and all sessions were videotaped and transcribed. Sessions where the therapists and observers had unanimously agreed that transformations had taken place were then compared to those where none had taken place. The sessions were analysed in terms of sequences of *problem elaboration episodes* where conversations included a statement of the problems and their causes. Subsequent responses by the therapist and the family were developed for each episode. The researchers developed a model from this analysis which consisted of three stages (see Figure 4.2). The first stage involved eliciting each family member's definition of the problems followed by an attempt by the therapist to promote a discussion of relational aspects of the problems and then a search for exceptions. In the second stage it was discovered that the emotional responses among the family members shifted, including statements about the positive attributions of child, recognition of the contribution of the family structure to the problems, leading to an ability to identify their strengths as a family. The researchers stated that:

> In all four successful transformation events, the task environment
> was marked by a shift in the affective tone from the original blaming
> of the identified child to a more nurturant or supportive position ...
> This final stage emerged not merely through an expression of emo-
> tion. Rather there was a sequential process through Stages 1 and 2
> where the affective responses gradually shifted to a more positive
> tone ... In each successful session, the shift to hope appeared asso-
> ciated with the expression of love and commitment.
>
> (Coulehan et al. 1998: 29)

They go on to describe how the therapists engaged in two important interventions to help promote this process. First, they responded to critical comments in a matter-of-fact manner. For example, in one session the parents
criticized their daughter for being too involved with her friends but the
therapist did not allow this to derail the discussion. Second, the therapist
invited family members to express their feelings, both positive and negative,
including feelings in the therapy session. They argued that this acceptance of
feelings and helping to process or 'catching feelings' in the room helped to
generate the emergence of a sense of hope in the therapy: 'The present study
suggests that shifts in family members' emotions may be underemphasized by
theorists ... the awareness and expression of emotion facilitate changes in
cognitive as well as interpersonal processes' (Coulehan 1998: 30).

The research by Coulehan et al. (1998) suggests important connections
between narrative therapies and attachment theory. As people tell their
stories they also express their feelings and these in turn shape the content of
the stories. As we tell a story of loss and misfortune we are likely to become
sad, and this feeling in turn may encourage us to focus on further details of
sadness and loss. In family contexts this can lead to other family members
joining in such an emotional amplification. Alternatively, people may
attempt to ward off the feelings that are arising by switching topics and
avoiding dealing with the issues. Coulehan et al. (1998) indicated that as
families were able to move with the therapist towards stories that were
transforming they experienced acccompanying positive emotions about
themselves and each other: hopefulness, relief and feeling more connected
with each other. There would be evidence of changes in behaviour and
communications, such as smiling, laughter, more open posture and so on.

Attachment theory complements such an analysis of narrative transformations in that it offers a model of some of the emotional processes in
families and characteristic ways of dealing with attachments issues. Johnson
and Best (2003) suggest that attachment processes are the key features of
family problems and the therapeutic process. She argues that one of the key
tasks in couples' therapy is to deal with significant emotional responses, what
she calls, 'catching the emotional bullet'. As an example, one person may

Stage 1: Individual family members express their viewpoints (old story is retold)

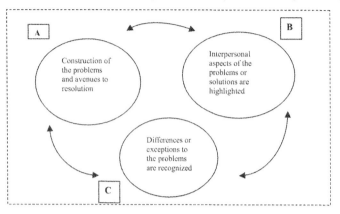

Stage 2: Affective responses among family members shift (new story emerges)

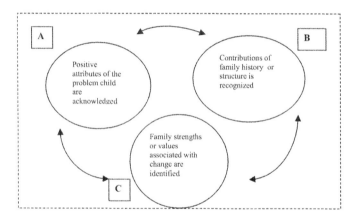

Stage 3: Hope or possibility of change is acknowledged

Figure 4.2 Transformation in narrative therapy

have risked making some personal admission, or apologized for some action that was seen as hurtful or disrespectful. Often such an admission or apology is not met with acceptance but with further criticism. A consequence can be that the first person feels stung by this further criticism, and humiliated and acrimonious withdrawal or counterattacks may ensue. The therapist may help transform this process into a more positive and hopeful experience by connecting with these feelings and emphasizing, for example, that this is the first step to change and the process of forgiveness. Coulehan et al. (1998) similarly pointed out that in successful therapy the therapist was able both to acknowledge the emotional expression made in the room and then to prevent the session from being derailed by negative expressions.

Narrative abilities

Narrative therapy achieves transformations through a range of sophisticated processes involving shifts in meanings and, as Coulehan et al. (1998) suggest, also through associated emotional shifts. As we have seen in the previous chapters, emotions and meanings are closely linked and the nature of early attachment processes shapes a variety of transformations of meanings regarding our relationships. A related question for narrative therapies is the extent to which they assume that people possess abilities or skills to place their experiences into narratives. The narrative therapies appear to be predominantly language-based and to require sophisticated narrative abilities on the part of family members. However, some techniques, such as externalizing, appear to work well with young children. An example is White and Epston's (1990) famous use of externalizing by using an imaginary character called Sneaky Poo with a 6-year-old child, Nick:

> Although Sneaky Poo had always tried to trick Nick into being his playmate, Nick could recall a number of occasions during which he had not allowed Sneaky Poo to outsmart him. These were occasions during which Nick could have cooperated by 'smearing', or 'plastering' but declined to do so ... In response to questions ... Nick thought he was ready to stop Sneaky Poo from outsmarting him so much, and decided that he would not be tricked into being its playmate anymore
>
> (White and Epston 1990: 46)

This quote suggests that Nick was able to remember incidents and people in the past and was aware of ideas such as tricking people and able to reflect that he was being outsmarted by Sneaky Poo. We can consider two bodies of evidence in relation to this question. The first comes from developmental narrative research which examines how narrative abilities develop in infants. The second from attachment theory which suggests that some fundamental narrative abilities, especially that of integrating experiences and being able to reflect on them, are shaped by our attachment experiences.

Narrative development

A growing body of research on how infants learn to describe their experiences suggests that it is highly complex developmentally. Habermas and Bluck

(2000) suggest that full narrative abilities develop as late as in adolescence. Young children like Nick, above, tend to have narratives which are more in the form of simple descriptions of events that have happened recently. Abilities to connect events over time into an unfolding narrative develop gradually and so young children offer descriptive accounts with relatively simple explanations of why people may have acted in particular ways. For example, when asked to tell a story about why someone acted in a particular way, preschool children describe themselves and others in terms of physical appearance and general evaluations such as 'good' or 'nice'. Young school-children describe people in terms of simple feelings, preferences and specific abilities such as, 'She's good at maths'. As in the example of Sneaky Poo, they may be able to appreciate that Sneaky Poo has played tricks on them and got them into trouble. Such a simple narrative does not require the child to consider complex narratives as to why his or her actions might be connected to dynamics and conflicts elsewhere in the family. Likewise, the frame can allow other family members to reduce self-blame and accusations.

Older schoolchildren are able to compare their own skills systematically with other children and to describe personality in more sophisticated ways using different habits and attitudes to generalize about others across different situations. In early to mid-adolescence this becomes more complex in that children develop the idea of personality as consisting of the integration of different emotions and motivations and use this to explain how people act in predictable ways. However, it can be over-generalized so that people are seen as 'cool' or a 'freak' or 'weird'. Later they start to understand the idea of there being competing and conflicting tensions within a person's personality and that others may be less aware of some of their intentions and motivations and so some of their own and others' actions may be driven by unconscious processes.

In this example the narrative therapy approach can be seen, perhaps fortuitously, to be developmentally appropriate. Possibly this reflects the intuitive skills that many therapists are able to develop that helps them to match how they talk with different family members to facilitate communication and change. However, it may be that there are times where assumptions are made about the abilities of family members to engage in narratives. Narrative therapies appear to possess little in the way of a developmental map to guide the therapist in what family members may be able to process in narrative terms. A related point is that the development of narrative skills in children requires practice and support from parents. Peterson and McCabe (1992) conducted a study which explored the influence of a mother's style of talking with her infants on the children's subsequent narrative development. Two of the mothers studied differed considerably in the kinds of questions they each would ask their 27-month-old child. One mother focused on context and causes (who, where, when, what and why) and the other emphasized elaboration and detail (what happened). In the dialogues that follow we see how Helen's mother focused on the orientation section of narrative while de-emphasizing sequential events, whereas Cathy's mother, while prompting for some contextual information, was more concerned with eliciting the temporally ordered events in the child's experience (the two girls are aged 31 months):

Helen's Mother (M) and Helen

Helen: I was playing and eating play
Mother: You were playing and eating. And *where* did you play?
Helen: In the room
Mother: In the room. *What* was in the room?
Helen: [no response]
Mother: *Who* was in the room with you?
Helen: Sissy
Mother: Sissy, and *who* is Sissy?
Helen: My sister

Cathy's Mother (M) and Cathy

Mother: You told Isabella a story about *what happened* to you. Do you remember?
Cathy: I hurt my arm
Mother: Do you know *what happened*?
Cathy: [no response]
Mother: Where did you hurt your arm? Where were you when your arm got hurt?
Cathy: All the places
Mother: Where?
Cathy: All the places, there, there, there, there. Everywhere!
Mother: But where were you?
Cathy: Uhmmmm, on a cliff.
Mother: Oh, and *what happened*?

(Peterson and McCabe 1992: 310–11)

The two mothers can be seen to differ in the extent to which they not only ask questions about context – where things happened – but Cathy's mother is more likely to intersperse such simple factual questions with questions about actions or episodes: '*What happened*?' When the children at 44 months spoke independently to a researcher to give stories about recent events in their lives (for example, both described an attack by a bee) there were marked differences in their abilities to tell a story. Helen gave lots of facts but these were not well connected over time and there was less explanation of why people were doing things. Cathy's story, in contrast, was organized in terms of offering several events that built up to a 'high' point, a focus and point to the story and then how events were resolved.

These studies offer a fascinating insight into the process of 'scaffolding' described by Vygotsky (1962) in terms of how parents help to support and build abilities for children. In the research by Peterson and McCabe (1992) it is possible to see how the complex skills involved in developing narratives is promoted by parents' questions and prompts. Also at times the parents offer examples of how to express events, offer reminders, provide factual clues to help and offer potential causal connections. Importantly, such activity takes time and requires the child and mother to be relaxed and feel relatively safe with each other. McCabe and Peterson (1991) also point out variations in parental styles that suggest emotional differences. For example, one style of parental elicitation was described as 'confrontational topic extension'. Here the parent frequently corrected the child's talk with a sort of 'get the facts right' approach. This resulted in the child becoming 'openly resistant' to telling their story. Another somewhat remote style was described as 'repetitive', for example, simply asking the child questions about things that the child already knew and the parent supplying little information or elaboration.

Defences and narratives

In the previous chapter we saw how research, especially on the AAI, indicates that powerful emotional processes are triggered when people tell the stories of their childhood attachment experiences. Attachment theory offers considerable evidence that the feelings aroused as we tell our stories also lead to various forms of transformation and so arguably distortions taking place. We have also seen that this can not just be due to internal processes or the internal working models that the speaker holds but it also resides in the interpersonal context within which the person lives. In effect a child can come to learn what is possible and appropriate to communicate with her mother, and how this might be different with her father and so on. Experiences of these different relationships can become generalized to a broader sense of what in 'general' is appropriate to talk about, and this includes what the person assumes is appropriate to say to an interviewer or therapist:

> the person comes to the interview with a life story already developed. The interview is designed to get at that story. But the interview is an interpersonal interaction itself, replete with demand characteristics and other situational factors that shape the account that is given in important and sometimes inexplicable ways
>
> (Baerger and McAdams 1999: 1135)

Baerger and McAdams (1999) emphasizes that narratives not only tell a story in terms of events and facts of our lives but they also embody defence processes whereby some features, aspects and events may be excluded or distorted. Freud has described a variety of defence mechanisms that his clients were seen to employ: denial, projection, idealization and intellectualization. These can be seen to operate when we tell a story about our lives, and especially about the more painful and potentially difficult aspects. However, this is connected to the idea that our narratives, whether we are talking to someone or our private thoughts, are targeted at an audience. Psychodynamic theorists (Freud 1961; Kohut 1977) had suggested that an important, internalized audience is our parents and central family figures. One sociological theory (Mead 1934) is that this can be a 'generalized other' – our internal representation of our cultural values and norms. As an example, Wiersma (1988) found in a study of women returning to work after lengthy periods of being at home with children that their initial stories appeared clichéd and stereotyped: 'press reports'. On further investigation anxieties and tensions became apparent and it became evident that the stories contained processes of denial and idealization which made it more possible for the women to cope with the anxieties of returning to work. It could also be seen that their stories were well-rehearsed and addressed to an audience of women who were influenced by popular feminist ideas of the joys of returning to fulfilling work from the oppression of family life:

> The audience consisted of other women in their cohort and those perceived to be part of the Women's Movement at the time of the study, many of whom shared the ... assumptions about gender equality, the oppression of domestic life, and the liberating power of paid employment. The press release was rehearsed and fashioned with respect to that reference group of like-minded women
>
> (Baerger and McAdams 1999: 1139)

Hollway and Jefferson (2001) have similarly described that narratives do emotional work for the speaker. The way we tell stories and the various defence processes that we employ help us to manage painful and difficult feelings arising from memories of events as we tell our story. As we develop into adulthood we come to hold ready-made stories about our lives. Sometimes we have told these many times to many different audiences. For example, as an 8-year-old child I left Hungary as a refugee in 1956. I have told my story many times and though I tell the facts pretty much the same way I will embellish some aspects in particular ways according to my audience. However, different responses and questions from listeners can still trigger me to look at the experience differently and even to remember some features that had slipped from my conscious awareness.

Baerger and McAdams (1999) suggests that defence mechanisms may operate because the person cannot identify an audience that will understand, sympathize with or approve of the story. We may assume for example that an important family member could not or would not understand our story. For example, a single mother may have devoted her life to raising her son and desperately wants his approval. He becomes her internalized audience for her story of self-sacrifice and she may find it difficult to contemplate telling another story of how he has disappointed her, or that she feels he does not care for her or even that she does not care for him. Defence in this way is a denying, or repression or cutting off, of parts of our experience or potential feelings because we think other important people might not understand. In addition we might anticipate or imagine and fear the consequences of their emotional reactions. Lying and deception might also feature as responses when we cannot imagine a way of explaining some actions to our internalized audience:

> The married woman who has built her identity around her family and set up her husband as the main internalised audience for her life story cannot incorporate the sexual affair she is having with a co-worker into her current identity. There is no story available for her that will make the affair understandable to her husband, and perhaps to herself as well. So she splits the experience off from the main story line of her life. In terms of defence, she may employ the narrative strategy of isolation or dissociation, establishing a separate line of storied experience that cannot, for the time being, be reconciled with what she fundamentally believes herself to be or to have been
>
> (Baerger and McAdams 1999: 1142)

Baerger and McAdams (1999) conclude that developing a life story is shaped by defence mechanisms and that these defences shape not only how a story is told but what stories are deemed tellable. This view connects closely with the idea that narrative therapy involves, and in fact requires, attention to emotional processes, and with work from attachment theory that has described how defence processes are shaped from early attachment processes in families. Moreover the process is seen as an interpersonal one with the defence process in our narratives being linked to internalized others and to interpersonal processes of how people respond to our attempt to explain our actions.

5 Attachment Narrative Therapy

This chapter draws together the discussions in the previous chapters to set out a psychotherapeutic approach which attempts to draw together systemic, narrative and attachment ideas. A central connecting theme from the previous chapter is that the process of change in both the narrative and systemic therapies involves an interaction between emotional and narrative transformations. The chapter goes on to connect this to the idea of therapy as a 'secure base' from which people become more able to develop coherent narratives. The chapter then goes on to outline how problems can be formulated from an attachment narrative perspective. A therapeutic approach is then outlined consisting of four stages: creating a secure base, exploring narratives, exploring alternative narratives and maintaining change. The chapter ends with an illustrative case example.

> Emotion is a leading element in a system that organises interactions between intimates
>
> (Johnson 1998)

In this chapter I want to weave together the strands from attachment theory, systemic therapy and narrative therapy to suggest an approach to therapeutic intervention with individuals, couples and families. I have called this approach Attachment Narrative Therapy (ANT) to indicate that it offers an integration of ideas from these approaches. Some very important and interesting attempts to integrate systemic and attachment theory approaches have been developed (Diamond and Siqueland 1998; Johnson and Best 2003). Aspects of these approaches will be outlined later but in addition I will be suggesting that ideas for the narrative therapies can usefully be added to an attachment/systemic approach. In particular, as we saw in the last chapter, transformations in narrative therapy, and arguably all the therapies, involve powerful changes in emotional states.

Systemic therapy and attachment theory

Johnson and Best (2003) argue convincingly that systemic therapy and attachment theory share many important features. To start with both approaches emphasize that circular processes are fundamental. The patterns of interaction between current attachment figures ongoingly confirm and maintain an individual's construction of an attachment relationship, rather than simply internal models from the past biasing present perceptions' (Johnson and Best 2003: 166). This suggests that both approaches can hold a focus on current, not just past, patterns of actions in families and other relationships. Feelings, behaviour and beliefs are being maintained by current patterns and as these change so too can the 'internal' attachment representations.

As we have seen in Chapters 1 and 2 Bowlby's (1969) initial view suggested that the child was predominantly responding to its parent in order to maintain a comfortable level of security. However, attachment theorists such as Kobak (1999), Bretherton (1995) and Oppenheim and Waters (1985) have argued that the process rapidly becomes an interactional one wherein the child is also influencing the parent. 'Attachment security results from a dynamic transaction between internal working models and the quality of current attachment relationships' (Kobak 1999: 39). In adult romantic relationships it is the case that each partner simultaneously offers and draws attachment security from the other. This can be seen as a circular process of mutual influence. Both attachment theory and systems theory emphasize that systems need to be flexible, adaptive and open to change. This includes being able to develop new ways of acting, viewing each other and solving problems. Kobak (1999) emphasizes that attachments should be seen in communicational terms not simply or predominantly as internal representations but as a pattern of communication:

> Open communication can greatly reduce the extent to which disruptive events are perceived as threatening the availability of an attachment figure. For example, a parental expression of anger can be perceived by the child either as a signal that the child needs to alter his or her behaviour to maintain a co-operative relationship, or as a rejection or threat of abandonment. When communication is open, parental anger is usually accompanied by an explanation that provides the child with a clear understanding of the specific source and context for the anger
>
> (Kobak 1999: 33)

Systems theory has from its inception argued that families need to be seen as communicational systems and how open and flexible the communication is is related to adaptive or 'healthy' functioning. Both attachment theory and systems theory can be non-pathologizing. From the outset Bowlby (1969) argued that the attachment patterns and internal working models make sense and fit in the context of the child's environment. Both theories also connect the internal experiences of family members with external events, interactions and communications in families. Some systemic approaches drifted towards a position which tended to emphasize pattern at the expense of internal processes. However, one of the seminal ideas was that of 'punctuation' (Bateson 1972; Watzlawick et al. 1974) which emphasizes the relationship between beliefs and actions (see Figure 5.1). Both partners may have developed fixed beliefs about each other and see each other in terms of fixed, essential traits, such as avoidant or critical. These beliefs may lead each of them to act in ways that serve to confirm the other's 'worst fears' and so they maintain the pattern. Though typically focusing on beliefs and cognitions, there is no reason why systemic theory cannot similarly conceptualize the patterns in terms of emotional connections.

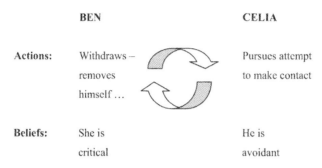

Figure 5.1 Cycle of actions and beliefs underlying an approach: pursuit cycle

Attachment theory holds a similar systemic analysis in that the parent and child or a couple hold each other in such cycles. It also emphasizes that these patterns are based upon fundamental attachment needs. Johnson and Best (2003) suggest that attachment theory makes an important addition to systemic therapy in emphasizing that in intimate relationships the attachment patterns are paramount in fuelling interpersonal dynamics. Interestingly, the example in Figure 5.1 is common to many distressed couples. Johnson and Best (2003), Byng-Hall (1980) and Pistole (1994) have described such patterns in terms of distance regulation in couples. Underlying such a pattern can be seen to be fundamental attachment insecurities: Celia, fearful of emotional abandonment, pursues Ben for emotional contact. Ben, fearful of such contact and the feelings that it arouses, seeks to withdraw. However, the withdrawal may lead to a critical attack by Celia who experiences the withdrawal as a rejection. The expression of distress, tears and anger may be experienced by Ben as an attack and consequently this leads him to withdraw further (Dallos and Dallos 1997).

Such analyses can also be applied to patterns between parents and a child. For example, a frequent pattern in work with adolescent children is one where the parents feel their child is secretive and he or she feels that they are unavailable (see Figure 5.2). The emotions underlying and fuelling such a

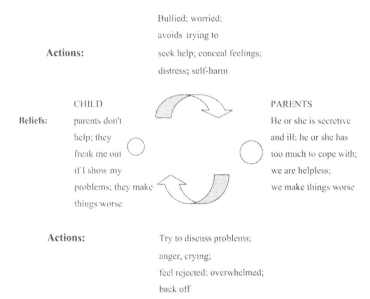

Actions:

Bullied; worried;
avoids trying to
seek help; conceal feelings;
distress; self-harm

CHILD

Beliefs: parents don't
help; they
freak me out
if I show my
problems; they make
things worse

PARENTS

He or she is secretive
and ill; he or she has
too much to cope with;
we are helpless;
we make things worse

Actions:

Try to discuss problems;
anger, crying;
feel rejected; overwhelmed;
back off

Figure 5.2 Cycle of actions, beliefs and feelings underlying a self-harming cycle in a family

pattern might be a feeling on the child's part that the parents are too distracted and preoccupied with their own problems and they are unable to help. Hence, the child may feel abandoned and angry and if the parents do offer some attempt to help they are rebuffed. For parents who are distressed and preoccupied with their own problems this may fuel a sense of failure which leads them to withdraw or be upset. The child may feel guilty and angry that he or she has upset them and feel worse. Systemic therapists have described such patterns but attachment theory adds that fundamental to these processes are the emotional processes and attachment needs.

Narrative therapies and attachment theory

In the example above we can already see that the patterns of actions and feelings are also shaped by beliefs and narratives. The narrative therapies suggest that the stories that we hold about our lives and experiences shape who we are, how we feel and how we act. In particular, problems are associated with stories that are 'problem saturated' – where the emphasis is on negative events, failure, dysfunction, helplessness and powerlessness. Often added to this are themes of irreversible damage or forms of inherited vulnerability or illness. Importantly, the narrative therapies emphasize that such beliefs, self-perceptions and narratives are transmitted and applied by family and other interpersonal processes but also convey wider culturally shared ideas. They may also be enforced by professionals who have power to apply such ways of defining people. Also, central to narrative therapy is the idea that therapy involves a process of assisting people in resisting such patholo-gizing processes.

A central contribution from attachment theory is that key to our experiences is the stories we have formed about our intimate attachment relationships. This is not to argue that these are the only relevant experiences. The narrative therapies have also offered an important political analysis of the destructive processes of poverty, oppression and pathologizing practice. At the same time research, such as Brown and Harris's (1989) study has shown that in circumstances of poverty and social deprivation one of the strongest protective factors is a positive, supportive intimate relationship. Having one or more secure attachment relationships was found to greatly increase resi-lience and reduce the likelihood for the women in the study of becoming depressed and seeking medication. This is not to minimize the effects of deprivation but to recognize, as much work using the AAI has also shown, that negative experiences in themselves do not invariably lead to problems. Being able to form a coherent story about negative events can contribute to the possibility of our being able to transcend them. This is also supported by studies by Harvey et al. (1992) which showed that an important feature of resilience in the face of trauma, such as sexual abuse, was a supportive figure who believed the victim and helped them to make sense of the events. For some of the women in the study this was a friend, family member or thera-pist. The most negative outcomes were for the women whose close attach-ment figures, for example their mother, did not believe or support them. However, it is important to exercise some caution here both for narrative therapy and attachment theory. Circumstances of deprivation, poverty and abuse do cause problems and therapy and social support of an intimate partner should not be used as an excuse for not engaging in wider structural changes and welfare policies. There may be a danger that focusing on nar-rative coherence can seem like a panacea to social problems.

Transformation of narratives also involves emotional processes. In the descriptions of the processes of 'problem saturated' narratives we can also see that the experience is profoundly emotional. A sense of hopelessness and helplessness creates an emotional state of arousal, distraction through phy-sical symptoms, irritability, sadness and so on which mitigate against the person or family being able to develop more flexible and optimistic narra-tives. The ability to construct new narratives requires that the relational, emotional base of a person's life is secure and open:

> A secure connection with others promotes flexibility and adaptation to the environment. Specifically, such a connection helps individuals to deal with their emotions in a constructive way, to process

> information effectively and consider alternative perspectives, and to
> communicate in an open, direct, coherent way with others
> (Johnson and Best 2003: 169)

Attachment theory therefore can complement narrative therapies in drawing attention to the emotional processes involved in constructing new narratives and, related to this, to what holds them in place. Research, especially from the AAI, also reveals that people develop styles of narrative which contain a variety of defensive processes. These can be seen as communicational styles in the family which may still be ongoing. However, they can also be seen as narrative styles, for example that a dismissing process leads to memories of past attachment experiences as well as the emotional features of current relationships being dismissed from the narratives. In narrative therapy a recognition of such processes can alert us to possible areas of mis-communication between the therapist and a client or family. It may also be the case that such an awareness helps us to refocus or alter the pace at which we approach talking about emotional issues. Above all else it may alert us to the important understanding that narrative therapy and placing their experiences into coherent narratives is a difficult activity for many of our clients. As Johnson and Best (2003) suggest, this activity requires a secure context where people can engage in the difficult process of integrating and forming new, coherent accounts of their experiences. They may need to learn gradually to change their characteristic ways of processing their emotional experiences.

ANT: attachment narrative therapy

Problems and difficulties can be seen then to involve patterns and processes in relationships which are interconnections of actions, narratives and attachments. Johnson and Best (2003) suggest that in working with couples there are 'only so many ways of dealing with a threat to the security of the connection with an attachment figure'. They argue that the possibilities can be summarized into three types of response: *escalation, minimization* or *denial* of demands for attachment with our partner. Perhaps such a view of the limited repertoire of processes is also then a testimony to the creativity of writers of romantic novels and poetry, plays and films? However, they do make the important point that there is a fundamental interplay between attachment patterns, actions and narratives. Elsewhere, I have described this (Dallos 2004) as constraints on choice, in that people can be seen to restrict their range of possible avenues of action by what they believe to be the only possible or permissible choices available to them. To paraphrase Karl Marx, people in relationships make choices but not in circumstances of their own

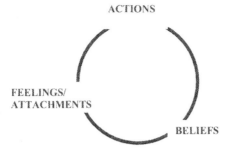

Figure 5.3 Core features of an attachment narrative therapy approach

choosing (Marx and Engels [1846] 1970). The interplay between attachment needs, actions and narratives can mean that each shapes and constrains, but can also liberate the other (see Figure 5.3). Difficulties and problems need to be seen in terms of this interplay between feelings, actions and narratives. In themselves these are not separate experiences or entities: when we act we also have feelings and thoughts (even if unconsciously), when we feel, we also act and have feelings and when we think and express our narratives to others or to ourselves we also feel and act. In fact talking to others invariably is a complex bundle of action, thinking and feeling. Memories and feelings are triggered, we gesticulate and give off, deliberately or otherwise, a whole range of communications, such as gestures. Recognizing this interplay of feelings, actions and thoughts is not exclusive to an ANT approach but the combination of these three offered by an integration of systemic, attachment and narrative perspectives does offer some new perspectives. Some core contributions will be described next. This will then be followed by an outline of how these ideas may chronologically follow in the process of therapy.

The therapeutic relationship: creating a secure base

A substantial body of evidence points to the importance, even the centrality, of the therapeutic relationship as the basis of therapeutic change (Luborsky et al. 1983). The roots of this idea are in psychodynamic theory in Freud's (1922) emphasis on the centrality of transference and counter-transference as the forces that drive the therapeutic relationship. From attachment theory we can conceptualize therapy as needing to create a secure base (Byng-Hall 1995). In fact the prospect of therapy (as we saw in the extract from the family in Chapter 1) can be seen to present a situation of threat and anxiety for families. How it is seen and anticipated and in turn what family members do to reassure each other about and during the process of therapy can be seen as embodying the same processes in terms of how they reassure and comfort each other in times of distress at home. Attachment theory suggests that core features of how families construct a secure base are:

> 1 Showing a recognition and acknowledgement of the cause of problems and distress.
> 2 Showing an appreciation of what this feels like – a mirroring of the feelings.
> 3 Containment – conveying that feelings, though sometimes painful and frightening, are manageable and will not overwhelm or drive away the parent.

This process of reassurance is also central to Rogers (1955) ideas of empathy and acceptance. The therapeutic relationship and a sense of safety in it is built by an acceptance of the person, their beliefs and their feelings. This is not to collude with the problems or the explanations but to demonstrate recognition. Attachment theory shows that parents and children and adult partners in secure relationships are able to express negative as well as positive feelings and are able to disagree with each other. There is an openness in the communicational processes such that negative feelings are not excluded and instead attempts are made to explain why people are feeling in particular ways. In effect because feelings are connected to narratives, they are given meanings.

Research on the therapeutic relationship has emphasized (Bordin 1979; Luborsky et al. 1983) that it is built on three main components: affect, goals and means. These three are interconnected so that by recognizing and acknowledging feelings the therapist is then more able to develop and clarify with a client or family the goals and means of the therapy. An awareness of differences in preferred attachment styles and the associated defensive strategies can help the therapist to negotiate with an individual, couple or family the goals and means in terms of what will be talked about and how it will be done. For example, the first session with one family was dedicated to discussing what we might talk about and how we might do this. In particular we discussed what rules we could agree on regarding when to slow down in order to take account of how people were feeling. The father appeared to have a style which was dismissive and the mother seemed preoccupied, the daughter, suffering with anorexia, demonstrated a style that appeared to contain elements of both. They explained that in a previous course of family therapy they had found the demand and the insistence of talking about painful feelings had been very aversive because the mother had become very upset as she remembered painful feelings, and the father had become angry about the expectations to talk about feelings as opposed to his more immediate concerns about his daughter's safety. The daughter in turn found the sessions aversive because she felt bad that her parents were being made upset because of her. We discussed how different people in the family preferred doing things and whether we could agree on some rules about how to do the talking. We agreed on a number of rules: people could stop the process if they were feeling too anxious and would signal this and I would look out for this on their behalf. People would talk one at a time (though the mother wasn't so sure about this) so that accusations and counter-accusations would be less likely. In the event the family members felt able not to abide by the rules all the time. I checked with them at various points in each session and at the end whether the pace, content and nature of the talking was acceptable and safe enough. They said that it was and that these sessions were comfortable.

Finally, attachment theory also connects with the concept of therapy as scaffolding. The research on the AAI indicates that people differ in the extent to which their narratives are coherent, show integration and are reflective. From the research on the development of narratives in children this can be seen as narrative abilities or 'skills'. This helps us to recognize that for many families the opportunities to engage in open communication and to have the support of parents to develop coherent narratives about their experiences has been largely absent. Hence therapy can be seen in a sense as having a supportive component in that we can offer scaffolding to foster these abilities. One central component of this is a context of safety and calmness which is a prerequisite for the complex process of integrating information and experiences held in the different memory systems. As Crittenden (1997) makes clear, such integrative processing requires emotional calm, we have to feel free from a sense of danger and threat. Where family members feel anxious, hostile and in conflict with each other rigid thinking rather than integrative processing is more likely to occur. Part of the therapeutic process therefore is to help people in this process. This can involve the therapist supporting family members' attempts to develop integration by offering encouragement and validation, offering possible narratives that family members can discuss, building or elaborating family members' narratives and helping them to complete their formative attempts at their own re-storying. In addition to this we can model the conversations whereby such development takes place, for example in reflecting conversations with other colleagues, self-disclosure and inviting family members to comment on their feelings towards the therapist. This can help both to model integrative processes and to elicit material with which integration can take place. Importantly it can help to make material about relationships and feelings available and suggest ways that this material can be integrated.

Formulation with an attachment narrative perspective

Central attachment patterns

A central feature of an ANT formulation is to identify and describe patterns of actions and beliefs in relationships that are fuelled by core attachment processes. Attachment, needs, anxieties and patterns are seen as the central driving energy of relational systems. As in the example of Celia and Ben above we can propose that the rigidity of the pattern is maintained by the attachment anxieties of each partner. This in turn fits with what each partner brings to the relationship from their own attachment histories in their families and previous relationships. Possibly Ben has learnt that he should not expect to rely on others, his needs will not be met and to express his feelings only leads eventually to disappointment and pain. For Celia, she may have learnt from her family that the only consistent way her needs will be met is if she continues to escalate her demands by showing her anger and coercing people to respond. Adults develop skills in disguising these patterns and they may not be evident early in a relationship, especially in the heady climate of sexual excitement. But they are likely to surface later when stresses, distresses and conflicts from within and outside the relationship arise. Ben may have had a humiliating experience at work which he tries to conceal from Celia, as is his pattern (dismissing) but nevertheless he cannot fully hide his sadness and distress. Celia may experience this as a rejection of her, again consistent with her pattern of closely monitoring people's feelings (preoccupied pattern), attempts to gain reassurance but perhaps in an angry manner which Ben perceives as critical. Each partner's core attachment patterns can be seen to fuel the cycle. It is not a question of having to label people with attachment styles but these can be used as a guide to thinking about what some of the emotional processes might be. Without this focus we might be able to describe the patterns but have little idea what is maintaining them or, importantly, how they have arisen in the first place.

Johnson and Best (2003) add to this analysis by suggesting that it is important to search for the heart of the emotional dynamics and to identify what they call 'attachment injuries'. These are memories of specific incidents that people often hold about their families and relationships where they felt let down, abandoned and which represent for them some significant turning point: 'I went down to Dad and he was like "Don't be stupid and go back to bed", and I had to go back to bed. And after that I didn't bother going to him. I would just bottle it all up and just not bother' (Cathy, Chapter 1). For Cathy, this memory of her father saying 'don't be stupid' seemed to represent a pivotal moment from which point she could not trust or depend on her parents to look after her. Narrative researchers have referred to such memories as nadir experiences – a significant negative experience that has substantial consequences in contrast to 'peak' experiences which have the opposite positive transformative effect. These moments may not appear all that significant to others but they contain or somehow bring together or perhaps confirm a growing sense of disappointment – a sort of the 'last straw' moment. Likewise, Barbara remembered a significant moment with her parents:

Barbara:	It was because you [Dad] had only full-fat milk and I watered it down and you said something like...
Dad:	A sarcastic comment...
Barbara:	Yeah...

Barbara, who had been suffering with anorexia remembered this incident of being accused by her father of being deceitful about her use of milk on her cereal. This represented a form of 'injury' for her in that she felt she had been trying to control her anorexia, but by this comment her efforts were discarded. Frequently, people report such incidents and say that at the time they had a numb feeling, almost like being physically wounded and could only later reflect on the 'damage' they felt it had caused. Frequently we may at the same time feel that we are making 'too much' out of something, that what we feel is disproportionate. Johnson and Best (2003) suggest that in attachment terms the events, though sometimes apparently minor, are so significant because they tap into core attachment anxieties. Perhaps such emotional flash-points occur in ordinary daily situations because it is precisely at these times that we lower our guard, are relatively undefended and expect to be safe.

Trans-generational patterns

A second important strand in ANT formulation is to explore problems in terms of patterns across the generations. Attachment theory suggests that we parent our children in terms of how we were parented ourselves. This transmission it is suggested is through our internal working models. As we saw in Chapter 4 (Fonagy et al. 1991a) the attachment styles of expectant mothers in the AAI is predictive of the patterns of how their infants will be attached to them two or so years after the birth of the child. This is not to suggest that we are simply blind victims of the patterns that we have acquired from our childhoods, more that we hold these experiences in our narratives about ourselves and others. The experiences are held in terms of how we see others and ourselves and what we expect emotionally from others and how worthy we feel ourselves to be of love and affection. Formulation in ANT therefore attempts to explore how the expectations that people hold and the stories that they have about their childhood experiences are being played out in the current relationships. This can allow for a position of therapeutic neutrality in that we can recognize the patterns across the generations rather than becoming caught up in inadvertently blaming or finding fault in what parents are doing. An important strand in such formulation is Byng-Hall's (1995) concept of corrective or replicative scripts. This suggests that people look back on their childhood experiences and transpose these into the future in terms of what they feel they want to repeat – what was good about what their parents did as opposed to what they want to change and do differently. This idea is similar to Kelly's (1955) idea of constructive alternativism, that we make choices in terms of contrast and Bateson's (1972) idea of difference.

However, in this process of considering corrective and replicative scripts it is also possible to formulate defensive processes, such as idealization. For example, a father may talk about how he inflicts physical punishment on his child because his father did this to him and he learnt about discipline and manners from this experience. But as the father talks further it may become evident that he is becoming emotional, or even tearful, as he remembers these painful experiences and the idealization process might then be revealed. He might start to be able to connect with how frightened his young son felt as he himself did at his father's beatings.

Organization of narratives

An ANT formulation includes a consideration not only of the content of people's narratives but how these are organized. This adds to narrative perspective which can be overly cognitive and overlooks structural features of our stories. A focal point is the idea of 'narrative competence' in that the formulation takes account of what experience people may have had in placing the past events in their lives into coherent narratives. With families we can look for what the current patterns are in terms of how family members talk with each other and try to find explanations for their problems and how these are connected with their relationships and emotional processes. At the broadest level we can describe this as thinking about the extent to which their communication can be open, but more specifically in terms of how it is organized around the two main attachment dimensions: restriction of feelings or restriction of cognition. For some families talking about feelings may be a difficult activity, for others forming structured cognitions may be difficult. Typically, there may be considerable differences in styles within a family. Part of an initial formulation may be that, as in the example of Ben and Celia above, their differences make it difficult for them to communicate with each other. In therapy this may point to some differences in orientations for each of them – a focus on opening up feelings and moving beyond cognition and rational explanations for Ben, as opposed to calming feelings and assisting in developing structured understanding of her experiences and relationship for Celia.

This formulation can be developed further by a consideration of memory systems and how defensive processes may appear to be operating. Especially in more severe problems, it may be the case that different experiences are held in different memory systems with a lack of integration between them. For example, painful or traumatic memories may be held in a sensory and procedural memory system, with intense imagery at times of repetitive patterns emerging. These may not be connected with a semantic or episodic memory system in which events are forgotten or where defended version of events prevail. Such an analysis connects with psychodynamic formulations but attachment theory adopts a systemic stance which looks for the patterns of actual events and interactions in the past that have produced these ways of processing the events. Further, the formulation looks for how these may be maintained in current patterns of interactions. As an example, for Louise and Mark the dominant story of their relationship difficulty was that Louise was sexually inhibited because she had been sexually abused by her father as a child. It had taken a long time for her to be able to reveal the abuse and when it came to trial at court the judge made some disparaging comments that partly discredited her account. Likewise, her mother had never truly supported her in her account of pain over the abuse. However, though Mark was sympathetic to this abuse he minimized the effects of their current relationship and his own behaviour, especially the fact that he had been unfaithful and at times been emotionally abusive. Arguably, Louise's perception of these more current abuses was being distorted and falsified just as her father had originally distorted the abuse in her childhood. Eventually, when Louise was able to connect her current memory systems of, for example, images and episodes of Mark leaving her on her own when she was ill, having a miscarriage, Mark going off with other women, which competed with a distorted semantic representation of Mark as being 'kind' and 'caring', she was able to make considerable progress. She expressed her anger at Mark, clarified that she did not 'really' have a sexual problem and even that she felt she had in fact largely resolved her feelings about her father. Subsequently Mark was able to look with her at their own relationship and eventually apologize for some of his behaviour (Foreman and Dallos 1992). Disconnections between the memory systems can therefore be formulated as shaped by previous as well as current processes. Similarly, Bowlby (1969) has described (see Chapter 4) how parents can in some cases subject their children to starkly distorted representations of events in telling them that what they have seen means something other than what their own sensory perceptions tell them they have witnessed. Frequently, as for Louise above, this can be when an abusive parent tells a child that sexual abuse was just loving stroking or a 'little massage'. In one family for example I was concerned when a father talked of 'tootsie' time, which involved massaging his daughter's feet, that this might have had denied sexual overtones (Dallos 2004) and that for example he might have been becoming sexually aroused during this activity. Interestingly, one of the tearful comments that his daughter frequently made in family therapy sessions was that people were lying, possibly an allusion to this activity and experience as well as other confusing processes in the family.

Emotional triangulation

In Chapter 3 we saw how children in families not only are influenced by the emotional relationships they have with each of their parents but also by the nature of the relationship between their parents. Further to this they are also involved in various triangular processes, possibly involving other siblings, grandparents and so on. The nature of the emotional relationship between the parents, however, is likely to be of primary significance and in effect the child has a relationship with the parents' relationship. In Chapter 1, Cathy poignantly described how her parent's relationship impacted on her: 'They won't argue while I've got this because it might make me worse. So um ... that's kind of bought, sort of like, I'm not in control as such but I've got more control over the situation that way.' Here Cathy is able to reflect on how her parents' relationship impacted on her but the emotional processes can be more submerged, for example where a child is emotionally drawn in to side with one parent against the other. There may be other processes whereby the child is drawn into secrecy and patterns of distortion or lying between parents which can become a pattern for how they manage their emotions. Cathy goes on to describe how being caught between her parents felt: 'I was such a daddy's girl, I really was. I used to feel so guilty, because guilt is such a huge emotion for me, and I used to feel really guilty that I'd spend more time with one than the other and when they would argue they'd always say, "oh she prefers you to me"'.

Other typical examples are scenarios where one parent instructs the child to keep a secret from the other parent about some action or event:

> Oh, she used to take me shopping every Saturday, for example, like we would go shopping every Saturday and she would um cut on the grocery bill right. And tell my father she spent £70 but she only spent £50, right, so we would pocket the £20 and we could both go and buy a dress. That type of thing
>
> (Crittenden 2004)

Or, there is a coalition formed so that a child is 'protected' against another parent in terms of some misdemeanour:

One day I got really angry and broke a wooden blackboard [that Dad had made for her] ... I was worried about Dad ... he's gonna smack me ... Mum just gave me a hug and said don't worry we'll fix it up. And that was our little secret like we fixed it up and Dad didn't even know

(Crittenden 2004)

Though these are common family patterns they offer the possibility of formulating attachment processes in terms of past and current patterns of triangular processes. They also indicate what patterns have been and may be in place currently that promote lack of open communication and deceptive processes. In particular they indicate how deception and lying becomes embedded in a family system and subsequently lead to a sense of confusion, lack of trust and insecurity – 'You cannot believe what others say and I'm not sure I can even believe myself.' Perhaps most importantly the triangulation processes mitigate against integration and coherence of narratives. Information in terms of what people have done, how they feel, their intentions and what they would do is restricted, distorted or falsified which makes it difficult to form narratives that are coherent – a little bit like trying to put a jigsaw together where the pieces keep changing shape, disappearing, are said not to exist or even when the message is that the picture that is supposed to be there bears little resemblance to what the pieces are suggesting is there!

A consideration of triangulation processes across the generations can therefore be an important and non-accusatory way of exploring the perceived costs for family members of being open and honest. This is obviously a complex issue when families are talking together and have to face possible recriminations at home after a session. Triangulation may also happen in individual work where the client may draw the therapist into the characteristic triangulating processes, for example eliciting the therapist to side with them against an insensitive, unfeeling, uncaring or abusive partner. In my work with adolescents it is very tempting to take the young person's side against their controlling, conservative, restrictive, abusive parents. It is often harder for the young person to reflect on their own role in some of the conflicts that arise and this may typically be a reflection of a similar pattern of triangulation at home where they conscript or are conscripted by one parent against the other.

Implications for intervention

Constructing a therapeutic relationship is in itself an intervention and arguably one of the most powerful aspects of therapy. Likewise, in the discussion of issues relating to formulation it is apparent that the questions that we might ask would also in themselves be likely to promote some changes, especially in how people see their relationships. An ANT perspective in addition suggests a number of points of focus for interventions including patterns of comforting, identifying key emotional moments and encouraging coherence and integration.

Patterns of comforting

Throughout our lives we need to turn to others to help us manage difficult feelings, problems, conflicts, distress, humiliations and anxieties. It is typical in family therapy sessions that members recount the problems, for example extended descriptions of what a child is doing wrong. In some cases, as in self-harming behaviours, there are dramatic descriptions of the details of the problems. It is clear in many such conversations that family members feel hopeless and helpless in the face of the problems. Frequently the problems have come to be seen as some essential quality existing inside one member of the family, for example a 'difficult', unmanageable child. An attachment perspective focuses on how family members have come to feel that they cannot comfort each other. Such a discussion is often difficult because moving too quickly towards it can result in parents further describing how all their efforts to help have been useless or have been dismissed. One helpful approach can be to trace patterns of comforting trans-generationally to discuss what the parents' experience of it has been themselves, what they have learnt from their own experiences. Often this reveals that the parents have themselves had little experience of having been comforted. Or, there are unconvincing statements that what they had was fine but very little evidence to support what this was. Such discussion requires that there is already a good therapeutic relationship in place or the members are likely to withdraw into a sense of being accused that they are inadequate because of their own upbringing. Alongside a trans-generational exploration it can be helpful to explore experiences in the current family, such as how they comforted a child or, for couples, each other, early in the relationship. This fits with a 'unique outcomes' or 'solution focused' approach that looks for previous examples of successes. It becomes clear in this exploration that many families have had to construct, piece together, some ideas about what it might feel like to be comforted.

In some families, for example where parents have been brought up in institutions, I have held conversations with them about how they have acquired ideas about how parents comfort children. This can reveal idealized versions of how this happens but also it allows for a sympathetic position to be taken with parents about how hard such an activity is if you are having to assemble the skill from books, magazines, films, television or what you have observed friends and others doing. This can lead to helpful discussion about how such learning needs to happen at an emotional and experiential level and offers a sympathetic position to parents on their good intentions and understandable distress when they do not understand why things are not working. In part the therapeutic relationship can itself be explored as part of this process, for example for the family to be able to comment on what the therapist does and what is or is not comforting for them. This can help to model and give practice of engaging in a similar process at home: the need to check out with their children what is helpful in a way that probably nobody did for them. These discussions can raise powerful feelings for parents as they remember their own attachment hurts. In one case a parent commented that just at the point where she felt close to her child and able to offer her comfort she remembered her own abusive childhood. This set off painful memories for her, so her behaviour towards the child changed, she withdrew and grew cold, which confused her child and led to distress and anger. This reaction then fuelled the mother's feelings that she was inadequate and failing leading her in turn to angry withdrawal from her child (see Figure 5.4)

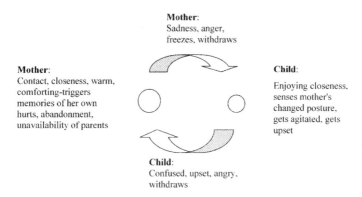

Mother:
Sadness, anger, freezes, withdraws

Mother:
Contact, closeness, warm, comforting-triggers memories of her own hurts, abandonment, unavailability of parents

Child:
Enjoying closeness, senses mother's changed posture, gets agitated, gets upset

Child:
Confused, upset, angry, withdraws

Figure 5.4   Intrusion of traumatic memories in a mother–child relationship

Identifying key emotional moments

Johnson and Best (2003) dramatically refer to this as 'catching the emotional bullet'. In work with couples and families, and also when individuals are recounting their stories of events, it is possible to identify processes where emotional changes are being attempted. For example, with Louise and Mark (earlier), Louise spent part of a session discussing with the female therapist how she had felt about her relationship and their problems, while Mark and the male therapist listened. She went on to describe how his insistence on sexual contact, even when she had been ill, had started to feel for her like rape.

After listening, her partner and I discussed his thoughts and feelings and he became tearful and apologetic that she had felt him to be acting this way. Though this felt like an important turning point and point of forgiveness, Louise responded by saying that she was not sure that he would ever really change his ways. When remorse is expressed it is not always acknowledged, as if the person who is hurt wants to hurt back. This can be a dangerous point emotionally since the temptation can be for Mark in this situation to perhaps feel hurt and retaliate, 'See what she does, she never forgives – oh what's the point in coming here'. Johnson describes how it is important to catch this moment and help people to discuss what the feelings are, what sense of rejection is operating, how hard it can be to forgive and that this will take time to happen, but small first steps can be taken. Connection with their own childhood attachments can also be helpfully woven in to discuss which of their own anxieties are activated in such interactions. Specifically, it can be helpful to locate what events are perceived as having led to the anger, loss of trust and feelings for each other – 'the attachment injuries'.

Encouraging coherence and integration

In the formulation with a family or couple we include a consideration of their narrative styles and, as discussed above, as a starting point we might consider whether their style is to organize in terms of a dismissive strategy: dismissing emotions and emphasizing cognition or a preoccupied strategy: dismissing cognition and emphasizing emotions. This is not a rigid typology or 'diagnosis' but a more or less helpful starting point that can allow us to adopt a compassionate approach, which acknowledges the difficulties and strengths that they may have in developing coherent and integrated attachment narratives. Recognizing the difficulties that people may have arising from their own family patterns can help in adopting a more compassionate stance, but it also indicates some possible initial orientations that we may adopt. Broadly the therapeutic orientation can focus on approaches to foster emotional expression or cognitive structuring (see Table 5.1).

The broad aim of encouraging expression of feelings is to help people get nearer to their feelings rather than taking the distancing position they have learnt. Mark (see Chapter 3) offers an example of a dismissive narrative style:

Mark:	I think tears were very frequent, but I probably ran to my mother, but I am guessing but I cannot remember. I remember cutting my hand badly on a shard of glass and screaming my head off and possibly running back home.
Int:	Running back home to your mom?
Mark:	Possibly, I can't remember

Table 5.1 Therapeutic approaches and attachment styles

DISMISSIVE	PREOCCUPIED
(Encouraging expression of feelings)	(Encouraging cognitive processes)
Enactment	Genograms
Role play	Lifestory lines
Reflective-functioning questions	Tracking circularities
Internalized other interviewing	Mapping beliefs, actions and cycles
Exploring areas of conflicts	Scaling questions
Managing conflict	Circular questions
Caring and comforting	Shared family beliefs

As we can see for Mark his memories of comforting are vague and hypothetical. Part of a therapeutic orientation to help him develop a more coherent narrative would be to access information about feelings. More generally, for people with a dismissive pattern, it may be helpful to adopt a broadly more experiential orientation using role play, suggesting enactments or demonstrations of emotional process, using empathetic questions (how others might be feeling) and internalized other interviewing (Tomm 1984). There can be an emphasis on exploring the emotional issues, such as how conflict is managed as well as caring and comforting. The aim is to help them to develop narratives which incorporate feelings and emotion and do not involve such a shut down of sensory and episodic memory systems.

In contrast, encouraging an expression of cognitions aims to assist people to gain some distance from the immediacy of their feelings and to be able to reflect on and develop narratives which can locate experiences in causal and temporal connections. Lillian (see Chapter 3) offers a flavour of what the narrative style might be like for people with a preoccupied pattern:

> Int: When you were upset as a child what did you do?
> Lillian: I don't know, I can't remember, I used to run away apparently, hum ... So it used to get quite bad, so I would have a tantrum, and I still have tantrums, yes I still do it, but [laugh] ... yes, I used to throw things, you know like a psychic child, but that's all I can remember ... remember once being, I used to run away but I always came back, run away through the back garden because I was very tiny and it was a small hole in the fence where the cats used to go out and I went through there ...
> Int: Do you remember how old you were?
> Lillian: Yes, and my expedition always ended up somewhere [laugh]

Int:	So, how old were you?
Lillian:	Yes, I was probably about 3 or so, and I remember once I rolled and rolled and could not stop because I was so tiny and it was very windy and I ended up at the bottom of the hill, that was one of my expeditions out, running away angry.

(Crittenden 2004)

For people with preoccupied attachment styles the emphasis is on strengthening semantic processes. This can include a variety of structured approaches, such as use of genograms and lifestory lines which ask people to locate key events in their lives in terms of time and place. This can help to build more temporal order to their stories so that they are less disconnected in terms of timing of events. Tracking circularities and mapping cycles of beliefs and actions can help to foster causal and temporal relations between events in their narratives. We can also include questions encouraging semantic descriptions about how other people see events, their beliefs and cognitions and circular questions which attempt to identify patterns of responding in their systems (Dallos and Draper 2005). Incidentally, we can see the interviewer perhaps attempting to introduce some cognitive coherence into Lillian's account by asking repeatedly how old she was when the incident she is describing took place.

It is interesting to note that this sort of shaping of our style to people's attachment patterns seems to occur almost intuitively. For example, reflect on your reactions to the transcripts in Chapter 3. A typical response is to seek to introduce some sense of order into Lillian's account as the interviewer tries to do by repeatedly asking for facts. Mark typically inspires strong feelings in us of wanting to help him to express what he feels, to help him move beyond his painful defence. However, the emotional processes can be very powerful so that we can become caught up in unhelpfully engaging with such patterns. For example without noticing it we may become over-rational and lacking affect in a session with Mark. In fact it is quite easy to start to think that things are quite all right – there is no problem at all and no need to worry – or to feel overly animated and emotional or chaotic and out of control with Lillian. This framework is not meant to be a rigid prescription. There may be times when it is important to validate both Mark and Lillian's styles and not engender anxiety by deliberately or inadvertently challenging their coping styles. However, a recognition of these styles can help us to be more flexible and creative in fostering a 'fit', in the therapeutic orientation and thereby more likely to be able to assist them to develop coherent narratives about their experiences.

Summary

In this chapter we have considered some of the features of an ANT approach to therapy. There has been an attempt to offer an integration of ideas from attachment, systemic and narrative therapy in terms of how they comple- ment each other. More specifically the connections have been developed in terms of some of the key orientations that have been developed in an ANT approach to therapy. The therapeutic orientations described here are not meant to be exhaustive but rather to be illustrative of some ideas regarding formulation and intervention that are emerging. The hope is that they inspire further creativity.

It is important to consider possible tensions and contradictions in this approach. To what extent can this approach be collaborative? Psychodynamic approaches have tended to take the position that clients may have 'blind spots', for example in terms of patterns of defences, and at times they may need to be led and cared for by the therapist. Leiper (2001) makes the point that collaboration is not always possible but is something that shifts and changes as the needs and awareness of the client alters. In some sense an ANT formulation can be seen as implying that the therapist has an awareness of the client's attachment patterns, which it may not be possible to share with them because they are defended according to their attachment patterns. However, this need not be the case. For example, we worked with a young man, James, who had been depressed and suicidal who reflected that: 'One of the things that I struggle with is that people seem to think that my not showing my feelings implies that I don't care or feel things'. James was an unusually articulate young man, but in general our experience is that it is possible to share with people our ideas about their attachment processes, especially how we think they may be dealing with their feelings and needs. As Crittenden (1997) points out, it is not simply that people need to shift their attachment patterns but rather that they are able to choose to use them as they think appropriate and not be blindly driven by them. Hence to reach an awareness of our patterns is part of the important process towards developing coherent narratives and being able to integrate our feelings. It seemed to us that James was now making a choice to stay relatively reserved emotionally but that by being able to reflect on his pattern he was also more in touch with his feelings. Hence a discussion about people's characteristic patterns can be helpful, and it is possible to work collaboratively. It is my experience though that one of the most productive ways of achieving this is through discussions of trans-generational patterns since these are less threatening and they gently allow people to reach insights about their family's emotional patterns. More broadly, the aim is not to propel people towards some normative position of secure attachment. Unfortunately, there is considerable movement towards such a position as can be seen in the use of the term 'attachment disorders'. To the contrary, Crittenden (1997) makes the point that in some circumstances it is quite dangerous to have a secure attachment process. It involves taking time to reflect on our experiences, feelings, reactions, contemplating the consequences of our actions on others and so on. In circumstances of danger this might be fatal. Alongside this there are significant cultural differences. However, that said, we also need to bear in mind that a close analysis of attachment narrative patterns can reveal some cultural myths. For example, it is unfair to expect, as is commonly held, that women are better at emotions and relationships. Given that they share the same kinds of attachment relationships as their brothers why would we expect this? Analysis of AAI transcripts indicates that apart from a superficial willingness to talk about feelings and relationships there is little in the way of gender differences in the deeper features of narratives, integration, reflective functioning and coherence between memory systems. The expectation that they are better at emotions and relationships can place further pressures on, for example, young mothers, to be able to manage complex relational issues when in their own families they have had little assistance to learn to do this.

In the next chapter we will look at the practice and process of ANT therapy with an illustrative case example.

6   The process of attachment narrative therapy

This chapter starts with an overview followed by details of the four stage model which summarizes an attachment narrative approach. Each stage presents a summary of how ideas from attachment, narrative and systemic perspectives can be regarded as contributing to building the therapeutic relationships, exploring the presenting problems, creating change and fostering maintenance of change.

Overview of an ANT approach

It is common to view the process of psychotherapy in terms of a set of distinct stages. This is usually seen as starting with an initial assessment stage in which evidence about the problems is gathered leading to a formulation from which directions for treatment are produced. Though this can appear to be a self-evident basic structure, in fact these stages on closer inspection are not usually easily distinguishable. Gathering information about difficulties can in itself be a powerful intervention. Asking questions is not a neutral activity and as information is gathered the questions asked can prompt new ways of thinking which can serve to promote changes in understandings. This view of therapy as an ongoing, recursive process in which exploration, formulation and intervention interweave is central to systemic and narrative approaches. Systemic therapies have employed the idea of progressive hypothesizing (Palazzoli 1978) to describe the process of formulation about problems as an ongoing recursive process. Later, along with the postmodern movement in systemic and other therapies, this was revised to be seen as a less certain and expert process of 'curiosity' (Cecchin 1987). This was seen to contrast with the scientific connotation carried by the concept of 'hypothesizing'. This position is similar to that shared by narrative therapies which suggest that therapy is a process of co-construction of meanings. Hence they do not regard assessment or formulation as distinct processes. Instead, from the very first encounter between therapist and client they see a process of mutual construction of meanings. As we have seen in Chapter 4 (Coulehan et al. 1998) it does appear that in narrative therapy, as in other forms of therapy, the therapist does at times direct the flow of conversation and employs the techniques that the therapist feels are appropriate. Furthermore, it is evident that like other therapies a central part of the process of change is shifts in emotional states.

Central to an attachment narrative approach is that the therapeutic process starts with building a relationship. The nature of this relationship shapes how people are able to talk about their difficulties and this in turn influences the formulations about the problems that develop. Formulation about problems can be seen as an interactive, collaborative activity that evolves as the therapeutic relationship develops (Johnstone and Dallos 2006). The therapeutic relationship can be seen as the context within which the therapeutic endeavour is possible. The process of building the therapeutic relationship and formulation can be seen as essentially interconnected activities. As we ask questions and share our understanding of a family's difficulties this in turn can strengthen the therapeutic relationship. As trust and a sense of safety develop a family is able to share more of their feelings and able to access more of their own beliefs and feelings which may have been submerged. Therapy can be seen then as proceeding as a joint journey of discovery (see Figure 6.1).

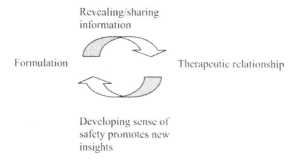

Revealing/sharing information

Formulation

Therapeutic relationship

Developing sense of safety promotes new insights

Figure 6.1 Therapeutic process and formulation

The stages in attachment narrative therapy model

Though therapy can be seen as an interactive process without discreet stages it can nevertheless be helpful to conceptualize it in terms of broad stages to offer a guide to assist our work. The four stages of ANT below are therefore intended to be a guide or a map that draws our attention to certain features that we might otherwise overlook. There may be overlaps between the stages and frequently we may jump between them within a session. We may even start the first session with an exploration of changes the family wish to make before much time has been spent on constructing a secure therapeutic base. What we do needs to fit with what the people who come to us want to do. Often families are eager to discuss what they can do to change things and want to explore these ideas almost even before they have described fully what the problems are. We may need to show that we recognize and acknowledge their desperation and eagerness for things to be different by engaging in such a discussion with them. Arguably, it is often just this that they want to communicate and for it to be acknowledged that things are desperate. Frequently, it is then possible to in a sense go back to the start and get to know a little more about the problems and to build the relationships. Though in an important sense we have already made a start in this by showing that we will listen and will pay attention to their concerns.

Stage 1: creating a secure base

This can be summarized as containing the following features. In practice we may not utilize all of these but they can help to offer some ideas about how we might start to build the relationship:

> - Talk about talk – what it is OK to talk about, explore family's rules and feelings, and what it is not safe to communicate about
> - Accepting stance, no blame, slow pace
> - Focus on competencies, externalize problems
> - Convey reassuring stance – therapy as containment – stance that can hold painful feelings, therapist(s) as being secure enough
> - Mapping the family support systems, professional systems
> - Being held in mind – attunement, reflect back that therapist understands causes of distress and how it feels, empathy

It may be helpful to illustrate this stage further by returning to Barbara and her family (Introduction):

RD:	What were your expectations of what this [therapy] would be like?
Tania:	I think we all thought it would be pretty stilted, difficult to talk and horrible long silences with everyone staring at their feet, waiting for someone else to say something and a wish not to expose any personal things…
Harry:	Being analysed I think…
Tania:	That's right, yes wanting to curl up and hide everything. That was what my view of what this would be like.
Harry:	Mine was we don't need this but we've got to do it because we have been asked … I must admit I have softened on that a bit since but that was my first impression … let's sweat it out.
RD:	What about you Barbara?

> Barbara: I thought it was a really bad idea, it would be awful and I wouldn't say anything at all. Being put on the spot and made to say things you didn't really want to. I just thought it would be really awful.

People come to therapy with a variety of expectations, feelings, anxieties and even fear. Arguably, the very decision to attend therapy in itself represents a substantial change for many people and it can be important to explore with them just how this has happened. In Barbara's family above we can see that their expectations were similarly negative and apprehensive. However, this is not always the case and for many couples and families there are often differences in what they expect or their willingness to attend. In some cases members talk of being 'dragged along'. For example a man comes because his partner wants him to, or an adolescent attends reluctantly because his or her parents insist on it. In my work, not infrequently an adolescent may refuse to attend as a statement of independence and perhaps as a way of communicating that his or her parents need to sort out their own problems and leave him or her out of it. Some initial discussion of how they have come to be there, including in some cases pressure from other professionals for them to attend, can help to start to build the therapeutic relationship. In work with young offenders, for example, it was important to signal my relationship to the criminal justice system. Youngsters were more able to trust me when I was clear about what aspects of our conversation I might have to reveal to others and what could remain confidential.

Overall it is helpful to adopt a position of openness in which we can discuss how we typically work, how other families with whom we have worked have felt and what rules we might develop about how we will discuss difficulties. Specifically, this addresses the idea from attachment theory that people will approach the therapy situation in different ways according to their dominant attachment styles. Hence, though there are some common approaches and activities that can help foster a sense of security, we can think from the outset about what might be particularly difficult or anxiety-provoking for people. For Barbara and her family, discussing feelings and problems clearly brought anxiety and was perceived as threatening. From initial conversations we can start to connect with a family's emotional styles and discuss with them what kind of activities we might engage in and how fast or slow we anticipate things will progress. In many cases this requires some element of guidance from the therapist since people are often driven to launch into detailing the problems. Very quickly arguments, blaming and counter-accusations can ensue, which can confirm a family's worst fears that this situation will be dangerous and not safe.

In common with systemic and attachment approaches a position of 'not blaming' is adopted. This can involve a discussion of what the aims of the meetings are about along with a clear statement that the sessions are not directed at finding fault and blame. Instead, that a focus will be on identifying strengths that they can draw on to help solve the difficulties. Drawing out a professional eco-map can be helpful to locate who else is, or has been, involved in assisting or treating their problems and what explanations they have been given. Most importantly this can also help to identify what has been helpful or otherwise about these involvements. This can also help to reassure families that they need not repeat painful unhelpful experiences and that they have control and hence can feel safe in this context (see Figure 6.2).

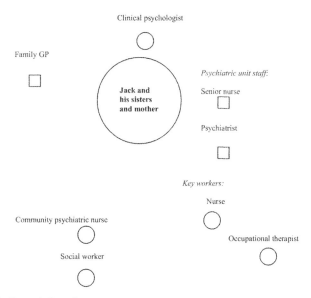

Figure 6.2 Formulation of an eco-map

In the example in Figure 6.2 from Jack, a young man who has suffered with 'psychotic' problems, it is easy to see that he has had and continues to receive input predominately from medical staff. The one exception is the clinical psychologist who holds the main psychological input and perspective on his problems.

The stance of adopting a conservative or even a paradoxical position regarding change can also be helpful. Emphasizing that we are not expecting changes to happen rapidly and that they can take things at their own pace can allow family members not to feel pressured into making changes or trying to see things differently before they are ready. However, it is also important to clarify that different family members may have different expectations and some may be desperate for things to move ahead quickly while others are more uncertain of what they want to change or the speed of change. It is helpful to state explicitly that we can negotiate together how quickly we can proceed and that this is always open for discussion. Alongside, and consistent with narrative and solution focused approaches, there can be a focus on competencies and what is working as well as a focus on the problems. This can help to convey an initial sense of hopefulness about the problems and also a sense that the therapist respects their strengths and abilities.

A key feature of building the relationship is that it mirrors one of the fundamental ingredients of secure attachments, which is that the therapist is able to show that she or he understands how the family see the problems and how they may have come about. Specifically this can be seen as connecting with their semantic representations of the problems. In addition it is essential to convey a sense of understanding on how this feels. This requires a reflection, or mirroring, of affect in showing that we also can feel how hopeless they might feel, how frustrated, angry or sad. It can be helpful too for the therapist to self-disclose about similar feelings and problems or to make connections with other cases to convey a sense of recognition of their views and feelings. Use of evocative language and reference to sensory images can also convey this sense of connection. For example, we can convey a connection with the family's feelings by use of metaphors and analogies on what they might be feeling, for example that it's the end of the line, they're feeling down in the dumps, blazing with anger, at their wits' end. In attachment terms this helps to engage with their sensory memory systems and the powerful feelings these often contain.

At the same time the therapist needs to convey that she or he can manage these feelings and is not overwhelmed by them. Giving time to a description of the problems therefore is important but it may also be helpful to intersperse this with looking at areas of competence to provide hopefulness and to start to convey that it is not inevitable that the problems will overwhelm them. The narrative approach of externalizing can dovetail into this discussion of problems by starting to consider the problems as external and not simply residing in family members as some essential quality. It can also foster a connection with the therapist in terms of promoting a sense of all working together to resist the problems. Again this can support a non-blaming stance that helps reduce anxiety and can foster a sense of safety in the discussions rather than a need to defend positions and actions.

Stage 2: exploring the problems

Exploration of the problems may have already started in the initial session or sessions, especially in terms of descriptions of problems. The focus in the exploration stage is on the emotional patterns that are underlying problems. The exploration is likely to proceed on the basis of discussions of problems and exploration of understandings about these.

- Processes current in family
- Explore beliefs about the problems and solutions: ideas about how to overcome problems
- Attachment patterns and injuries
- Triangulation processes
- Representation: memory systems memory systems and types of problems; individual vs relational; explore styles
- Affect regulation: comfort
- Trans-generational patterns: childhood memories
- Integrative questions: what have they learnt from the experiences?
- Encouraging multiple descriptions

Typically as people do this they also demonstrate their attachment patterns. For example, in Barbara's family the discussions were logical, rational and cognitive but devoid of feelings, and especially of statements about how people felt in relation to each other. This suggested that these areas were difficult for the family and that the exploration might need to proceed at a safe pace. One way to assist this is to ask people if the kinds of questions that are being asked are alright, whether they make sense, whether they want to talk about something else. This can be conducted without necessarily colluding with an emotionally dismissive process. We can, for example, at the same time gently enquire how people are feeling throughout this process and later comment on what defensive processes might be in play. This acknowledgement of the difficulties for them and invitation to reflect on this can for many people be a new experience of being emotionally looked after. It may offer a different way of relating which in itself may help in promoting some change. In effect it suggests that the therapeutic alliance is a powerful intervention in giving experience of a different, emotionally attuned way of relating to another person.

A broad orientation to the exploration is also to try and adapt not only to the overall attachment style of a particular family but also to differences between family members. This may mean encouraging different activities for various family members consistent with their narrative styles. Use of sensory materials, pictures, role play, drawings, viewing videotapes may assist people with more dismissive styles. The images may help to prompt feelings and emotions so that these can be accessed and discussed. In contrast, with pre-occupied orientations it may help to 'take the heat' out of the exploration by structuring the conversation, use of genograms, drawing out circularities and use of lifestory lines to map when events occurred. For example, in some families where emotions and their expressions are very raw and immediate it can be helpful to agree on a rule of 'one person talks at a time', or to engage in structured conversation so that, for example, the man in a couple talks with a male therapist while his partner listens with a female therapist and vice versa.

This can help organize and structure the conversation and allow people to semantically process what is being said instead of too rapidly getting caught up in an 'emotional whirlpool'.

Exploration of triangular and relational processes in general can be assisted by use of circular questions. However, these can have the added focus of exploring not just actions and beliefs but, importantly, the core feelings. For example, how does Barbara feel when her mother and father are arguing about her food intake? How does Cathy's mother feel if she sees Albert being close to her and comforting her? This exploration can help to reveal some of the patterns of secrecy, emotional deception and defences. The questions can also start to open up ideas of what would be different and how people might feel differently if it became possible to be more open and discuss their feelings rather than believing that they have to conceal them. Such discussion can be very liberating for children who feel caught up in endless and relentless conflict between separated parents. One young man explained that he felt that he had to watch very carefully what he said as he moved between his separated parents' households. He eventually came to recognize that this fear of saying the wrong thing might have contributed to him becoming mute. It was best to say nothing and have an the excuse of an illness for this than to say the wrong thing and risk upsetting one or the other parent by appearing to agree or sympathize with the other. Not surprisingly this young man also displayed anxiety-related problems, though it was very hard for the parents to see how these connected with their conflicts. Acknowledging this was especially difficult for the mother who herself suffered from anxiety and was having cognitive behavioural therapy (CBT) to help her deal with this. However, this appeared to further reinforce a belief that anxiety resided in the person, in her and her son, and was not related to interpersonal processes.

This therapeutic stance to exploration also connects with the exploration of patterns of comforting. Frequently family members describe the problems and their helplessness but do not articulate how comfort is given and used. One of the most powerful but also containing ways of engaging in this exploration of processes of comforting can be through an exploration of transgenerational patterns. It can be threatening for a family to discuss, for example, how they comfort a daughter who is self-harming or has been suicidal, since it suggests that they have failed in this. However, exploring relationships in the previous generation can move into a more general discussion of comforting in terms of how the parents experienced it themselves, what their expectations are and what they expect to receive themselves. This can connect with the externalizing framework of how family members can reassure and comfort each other to help each other work together to resist the problem. Frequently, this reveals that the parents have themselves had little experience of being comforted as children and have had to find ways of learning how to do this. Also, often they are unable to comfort each other as a couple.

An important part of the exploration can be an identification of 'attachment injuries' or memories of abandonment, hurt and rejection. As we saw in Chapter 5, people often have memories of some specific incident, episode or even period when the 'damage' was done. For example, Cathy recounted her father telling her 'not to be stupid' when she was upset thinking about her mother. Evoking such memories can be painful and there is a danger of defensive counter-accusations. Having a structure, such as one person talking at a time, can help people to have their say and for others to listen properly. This can allow others to hear the hurt as well as the accusatory part of the story. Eliciting these stories and helping them to listen also implicitly conveys the message that this can be safe, containable and that it can help to further their understanding of each other's feelings. In effect it helps to challenge a powerful and often destructive communicational rule that it is too dangerous to talk about these things and negative consequences will inevitably follow if they do talk about them.

Again this discussion can be guided by an awareness of family members' attachment styles. People with a preoccupied style may become very tearful and emotional at these memories, whereas a dismissive orientation can lead to denials that missing such comfort in childhood had any impact on them or to the problems now. The exploration can then be interspersed with either some focus on making sense of these events and relating them to patterns of actions in the family now and giving them a semantic structure, or the focus may be on contacting their feelings and making connections with these early experiences to provoke current feelings, for example, of anger about the problems. Children can listen while parents discuss their own relationships with their own parents. This can lead to a discussion of corrective and replicative scripts – what did they learn and resolve to do the same or differently with their children? This helps to connote their current styles in the family in positive terms. For example, if the parents describe how they wanted to repeat aspects of their own childhood experiences – a replicative script – this can be connoted as well-intentioned. Likewise, if they describe wanting to do things differently – a corrective script – this can also be viewed positively. Either way, it allows a framing of the parents' *intentions* as positive in terms of trying to do their best to do things well for their children. This can free parents up to then discuss how things are working in the family. Often the parents, through this trans-generational discussion, volunteer their own views about what is, or is not, working currently. Engaging in abstract conversations about relationships and feelings may be difficult for some families, especially those with a dismissive narrative style.

Stage 3: exploring alternatives – and change

By implication some of the exploration processes in stage 2 will have promoted some different ways of seeing problems and of acting. However, in this stage the therapy builds more on the security and safety established in the therapeutic relationship to explore different attachment narratives and attempt changes through:

- Developing a relational attachment framework
- Restorying attachment injuries
- Considering and enacting open attachment communication
- Encouraging multiple descriptions
- Encouraging reflection – experience of the therapy
- Exploring corrective and replicative scripts
- Exploring hypothetical, future-oriented attachment narratives

An important connection with narrative therapy is the exploration of unique outcomes. In ANT this focuses on unique emotional outcomes, for example times when the family members have been able to comfort and reassure each other. In particular this can focus on 'attachment injuries' and explore exceptions – whether there have been times when a similar need was expressed and the person confided in did respond in a way which offered comfort. This activity can itself generate powerful feelings and as Johnson and Best (2003) describe there can be emotional attacks which the therapist can help to process. This can involve enactments so that a couple engage in a different way of responding, for example trying to accept each other's apologies. Along with this they can be assisted to elaborate a future oriented story about how it might be possible to deal with each other's need differently in the future when these needs and conflicts are triggered.

More broadly this stage is oriented towards developing a relational attachment narrative regarding the problems. People are encouraged to link the problems with the relationship dynamic. In narrative therapy this is described as mapping the influence of the problem on persons, and of persons on the problem. More specifically for ANT this involves an emphasis on the impact of the problem on feelings and of feelings on the problem. In turn this can take place alongside a consideration of trans-generational patterns of how people responded to problems in the previous generation and what the emotional responses were, for example, to avoid or to become overwhelmed. Patterns of comforting can be considered here too, for example use of self-medication through alcohol or drugs. Alternatives can be explored, such as whether it is possible to manage difficult feelings with the help of others and how they might be able to engage in this. Family members are encouraged to clarify what they need from each other. For example, one young woman explained tearfully to her parents that she wanted them to acknowledge how hard she was trying to overcome her anorexia. She was also able to say that her mother becoming tearful all the time and her father getting angry was not helping. She wanted them to back off and let her get on with managing her eating but she did want their recognition of herself and her efforts. In fact she explained to them how she was deliberately becoming more sociable and finding friends so she would have other people to talk to, have distractions and support to help her feel better and fight the anorexia. She was able to say that acknowledging this rather than berating her about her eating was what she needed.

The discussion of trans-generational patterns in stage 2 can be continued in starting to explore in more detail alternatives that may be possible. As stated earlier, one very helpful feature of such a conversation is that it offers a positive connotation either way: if parents wanted to replicate then they were doing this for the benefit of their child and likewise if they were trying to do things differently. We can then ask questions about how this is working, which can allow parents to admit that it may not be working as well as they hoped. The children listening to this conversation can also see that their parents' *intentions* are positive and it can also be much easier for them to contemplate changing some patterns to a position of acceptance and safety rather than a sense of attack. These conversations can be structured in various ways. Children can listen while parents talk about their own childhood relationships with their own parents and draw parallels to current processes. The children can then be invited to reflect on what they have heard. With older children they can be asked to think hypothetically and consider what they might say in this situation in the future if they were parents themselves. The discussion can also include how their parents offered comfort and how they might have dealt emotionally with the kinds of problems that the current family is facing. This discussion can also reveal the current attachments, for example with grandparents, and how not just their ideas but their presence and relationships with the parents and grandchildren are having an influence.

A couple could take it in turns to listen to each other as each explains what they hoped to repeat or do differently in their own relationship. They can then comment on what is similar and different. Sometimes this discussion is in relation to previous romantic attachments, such as a difficult previous marriage, and what they hoped would be different in the current one.

The discussion of alternatives can be fostered by the use of circular and hypothetical questions, for example what the consequences might have been if the parents in the family had been treated differently by their own parents. The children can be invited to comment on what they see as the generational patterns and how these might change and what would need to happen for this to be possible. Such discussion can also be located in a historical context, for example in terms of different expectations about parent–child relationships, openness of communication, ideas about discipline and sexuality. This can allow a consideration of alternatives or in some cases some resolution or clarity about how such ideas shape the parent's emotional responses.

Finally, a guiding aim of this stage is to foster the potential to develop coherent and integrative narratives. The consideration of alternatives, of trans-generational patterns and enactment of different emotional patterns, helps to reveal or raise to consciousness material upon which more coherent narratives can be built.

Stage 4: integration and maintaining contact

> * Reflection and integration of the therapy experience
> * Anticipating relapse
> * Future support
> * Negotiating contact – separation from the therapy

This stage emphasizes a focus on integration and a continuing exploration of how emotional experiences from the past have shaped their patterns of comforting and communication. Increasingly this can involve reflections of the process of therapy itself and what has been learnt from it. The discussion can also focus on the future and what problems may arise and how the problems may show themselves again. It also involves a recognition of relationships and family life as inevitably requiring emotional processing. The discussions can include a focus on how problems can be tackled in the future. It can also be helpful in this process to reflect on what their emotional patterns have been in the past. This can include a realistic appraisal that they may choose to return to some of these patterns and what circumstances might provoke, for example a return to people keeping their feelings to themselves. However, a meta-awareness of these processes may mean that they are able to take some action to avoid problematic behaviours and feelings emerging again. Perhaps one of the core features of this stage is to examine excessive optimism or minimization of possible future problems. This may indicate that there has yet been little integration and increase in reflection.

Fostering integrative processes involves continuing the focus on reflection, especially about each other's emotional states. At this stage this can also turn towards hypothetical or future-oriented reflections about how people may feel in the future, how their relationships with each other may develop and change. An exploration of transition can be helpful, for example how different people might feel when the last child leaves home, at retirement, the arrival of grandchildren and so on. Importantly, this process also encourages an explicit elaboration of attachment narratives in terms of the future.

For many families establishing a trusting relationship with the therapist and the team has been a major task and change in their typical patterns. Many have also experienced an endless procession of broken attachments with professionals who have come into their lives, made promises to 'help them' and then disappeared. It is important not to continue this cycle, which fosters despair and lack of trust. Termination of therapy therefore needs to be collaborative. In some cases it can be phased out gradually but with some contact by phone or writing maintained to communicate that the team is continuing to hold the family in mind even if they do not still need to meet.

7 Case study: Cathy and her family

This chapter takes a detailed look at the case study of Cathy and her family in order to illustrate an attachment narrative therapy approach. The presenting problem was anorexia for this young woman, though a range of other problems emerged in the family. The therapeutic work described consisted of work as a family with the marital relationship, with each parent–child pairing and also individual sessions with each of them. The therapy is described in terms of the four stages: creating a secure base, exploration, exploration of alternatives and change, and integration and maintaining contact. However, in practice the stages overlap and do not invariably follow each other sequentially.

I worked with Cathy and her family clinically over a period of two years and in addition they also volunteered to be a part of our research sample. I thank them for their generosity in letting me use their material and for the great deal that I have been able to learn from them. I view their family with great affection and am delighted that Cathy is currently doing very well.

Cathy was 16 when we first started to work with her family. They were referred by their GP via the CAMHS (Child and Adolescent Mental Health Services) to a specialist out-patient eating disorder service that was attached to a local in-patient unit which included a specialist service for young people suffering with eating disorders. Following some initial meetings with them here, work continued in a community service away from the unit, though Cathy continued to attend for medical input and some individual therapy.

Cathy was a bright, vivacious young woman who was suffering with anorexia. Her weight loss was not so extreme as to warrant an in-patient admission but she was attending an out-patient eating disorder service. She had become physically ill enough on a number of occasions to warrant a brief admission to a paediatric ward. Cathy was currently attending school, coping socially, had been achieving reasonably well in her school work and was intending to go to university.

She was living at home with her parents (Albert and Mary) and one of her older brothers who quite frequently worked away from home. Her two other older brothers had left home. The family had moved to the region with Albert's job some 30 years ago, before the children were born, and this had been quite a substantial social change for them. Mary had also worked and this had been in a shiftwork system when the children had been younger, which meant that she had often been away from them in the evenings. Albert's parents were both dead, his father having died 15 years before and his mother 10 years before. Mary's mother was still alive and there was regular contact between them. Her father had died 15 years before.

We first saw the parents and Cathy together. Cathy's brother who lived with them did not want to attend sessions and Cathy and her parents did not wish to involve him. They did emphasize though that he was concerned and was eager to help Cathy to get better. The background information offered some comments regarding the family relationships in that Cathy's mother was described, by the psychologist working with Cathy, as being very concerned and worried about her.

Creating a secure base

The family came into the first session and Cathy sat between her parents. Our first impressions were that Cathy appeared the most animated and Mary communicated a heavy sadness in her manner and her withdrawn posture. In contrast Albert conveyed a sense that his role should be to remain calm and strong for his family. Cathy was the most emotionally present, confident, occasionally smiling and making eye contact with us.

We started the initial meeting with Cathy and her parents with a brief introduction to the team. Details of the 'technology', videotaping and live observation was explained, with a clear statement that we respected their choices and they could change their mind about how to work at any time. The parents expressed that they would 'try anything if it helped' Cathy, who also had no objections. Mary appeared the most uneasy about this so we explained that even though they had agreed to this way of working we would respect their wishes if they changed their minds later. Also, they could take the video away with them or ask us to delete a session if they did not wish it to be kept. There is a fine line at this early stage between helping families give an informed consent and raising undue anxiety by over-explaining the working context. We find it useful to draw a balance by suggesting that we try out how it feels in the session and this can help decide whether working with teams, the reflecting processes and video is helpful and comfortable for them.

There followed a discussion of the aims of the sessions and we emphasized that our view of meeting as a family was to elicit everyone's ideas and to try and find ways that we could work with them to help deal with the problems they were facing. This rapidly led to Mary explaining that she felt at her 'wits' end' and did not know what to do for the best, that everything she was doing seemed to be wrong. We acknowledged that this must feel very painful for her but that it was not the intention of these sessions to cast any blame.

Also that in our experience what seemed to help was finding ways to work together, especially since in our experience with other families anorexia was very powerful in dividing family members, leading them to feel worse, all of which allowed anorexia to gain an even stronger hold over them all. Adding to this *externalizing* framework we added that although we really understood that they wanted things to change, and likewise we hoped that changes would occur, this might take some time. Throughout this initial discussion we paid considerable attention to how they were feeling and invited each of them to comment on this.

Families are often very keen to launch into a description of the problems and when Mary started to do this we listened and then emphasized that we understood how concerned she was but enquired whether before we went further into this we could discuss how we would work together. It can be helpful at this stage to draw out an eco-map of the professional system in which the family is located. This helps not only to provide information about the network of involvements but also indirectly can help to slow the therapy to a safer pace. An ANT approach recognizes the strong emotions that are quickly evoked and tries to weave together and establish a pattern whereby the discussion can alternate between discussion with a structured, semantic focus and one with an emotional one (see Figure 7.1).

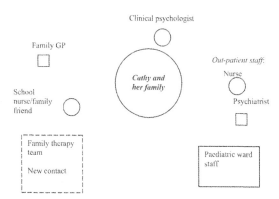

Figure 7.1   Professional systems eco-map

This revealed that most of the input, with the exception of the involvement of the clinical psychologist, had a medical orientation. This facilitated a preliminary discussion of what ideas they had gained from these inputs and what, if anything, had been helpful. We also discussed how our work with them as a family might connect with these other approaches. Mary said that she did not really know what ideas they had got but that she had picked up that it was an 'illness' and that it was her fault. Albert offered that they had not really learnt much about what to do to overcome the anorexia. Cathy said that she was finding the input from the psychologist very helpful and was understanding that the problems were not all about anorexia and eating.

This activity can help to set out what the family work can be about and also how it might connect with other pieces of work that are going on, for example how the medical issues can be monitored, and also to clarify how much of that needs to happen in our sessions. This can then offer a useful discussion of how our sessions might be different from these other inputs. It can also help pave the way for a more productive discussion of the difficulties. Also, it can help to clarify what features of these other inputs have been useful and helpful and what aspects of them we may want to continue in the sessions with us.

In particular we stated that very often we find with families that we quickly enter into a discussion of the problems and family members start to feel bad. Often they feel that they need to carry on talking about the problems and painful feelings because we want them to and misunderstandings start to develop. We therefore discussed how we might be able to develop some rules and signals about how people are feeling and how we can stop and take an 'emotional breather' if they need to. Also, how they can tell us if we are pushing them too fast or delving into areas into which they are not yet ready to go. We agreed that the therapist would make sure to check regularly how people were feeling, that people would say if they were feeling upset and even that people could leave the room for a time if they needed to. An idea borrowed from Haley (1987) also appeared helpful where we also drew up an agreement that to start with people would talk one at a time, and explained that otherwise emotions could escalate before we had a chance to hear and understand what each person had to say. This request can additionally implicitly suggest some thinking about how emotions are driven by interactions rather than by essentially internal states. Sometimes family members are very keen to cut across, interrupt, confront, contradict, accuse and blame each other as this conversation starts. For some family members allowing each other to have their say is in itself anxiety-provoking. There can be fears about what people will say and an anxiety, especially for the person in the 'peace keeper' role, that if they do not step in someone will say something dangerous and people will be held responsible for this later. Hence, some discussion of what it felt like to have each person have their say can also be helpful at this stage. Again, this is within the frame that we are not forcing them to do this but that we may make suggestions about managing the flow of the conversation from time to time. It is emphasized that the family can at any stage comment on our suggestions and ask to do things differently.

Such 'talking about talking' and setting rules of emotional safety can be helpful in delineating the context as safe as opposed to risky or as out of their control. Typically families appear to feel safer after such a discussion and proceed to enter into discussions about more difficult issues fairly rapidly. If we feel this may be going a little too fast, for example if one or other member appears to be becoming distressed without the others noticing or taking steps to assist them, we may suggest some slowing down and exploration of how people are feeling. As with all forms of therapy there is a fine balance between allowing families to explain what their concerns and worries are so that they feel they have been heard, and becoming drawn into 'problem saturated' descriptions. Moreover, as in Cathy's family, the person identified as having the problem can feel increasingly blamed and as causing all of the distress – generally and 'here and now' in the session. We interspersed the explanations of the problems with some solution-focused conversations about their occupations, interests, each person's strengths and any pleasurable activities in which they were still able to engage – 'despite the anorexia trying to stop them'.

A core of an ANT approach is that in the discussion of the problems we listen closely to what each member of the family has to say about the problems and we attempt to show that we understand both their views and explanations and what they feel about the difficulties. Mary did appear to find listening, especially when Cathy spoke, to be difficult and seemed to find it very hard not to respond emotionally, often becoming tearful. She was very sensitive to any hint of criticism from Cathy and would repeatedly appear distressed and tearful saying that she felt she had 'done it all wrong'; 'it's my fault'. In the first session a pattern started to become apparent where Cathy would reassure her mother and then become distressed herself and cry with her mother. Albert would look lost and look to the therapist as if to say, 'See what happens, what can I do?'

The first session in effect centres on connecting with the attachment issues for the family members and the therapist reflects back an understanding and acknowledgement of the pains they are experiencing. We also start to see some of the attachment patterns for each member and how these blend together in terms of how the family functions emotionally.

Preliminary formulation

Attachment issues for each of the family members
It appeared from the first session that Mary felt she was at fault, had somehow caused the problems and was therefore failing as a mother. She seemed sad and weighed down with life and gave a picture of being an unhappy woman. We speculated about her own childhood and suspected that she had unhappy memories and had been unable to resolve or move beyond the underlying experiences. Her attachment orientation appeared to be a preoccupied one. Her frequent crying and demeanour suggested that her feelings were very immediate, overwhelming and that she was engulfed by feelings of self-blame and sadness. Albert in contrast presented a picture of someone attempting to

put a 'brave face on things', of trying to 'look on the bright' side and to be strong. We speculated that his early experiences may have led him to adopt a role of carer in his family and suggested a more dismissive attachment position. Cathy on the other hand appeared to be more in contact with her feelings and seemed to present something that was both a blend of her parents' attachment styles but also indicated a more balanced attachment orientation. It also appeared to us that she did not feel secure that she could rely on her parents for support.

Relationships and attachment

The relationship between the parents appeared emotionally distant. There was little eye contact, emotional mirroring or any support of each other's positions. Mary was quiet when Albert talked but did not respond to what he had said. In contrast Albert seemed anxious when his wife spoke and was subsequently appeasing in following her line of conversation. It appeared to us that their relationship might have a central element of a pursuit–distancing cycle with Albert appeasing and trying to be close to his wife and Mary distancing herself and withdrawing (see Figure 7.2).

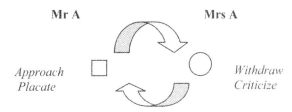

Figure 7.2 Placate–criticize cycle

The clearest pattern of emotional contact appeared to be between Cathy and her mother. It appeared that Mary was asking for support and validation from Cathy who seemed in a reversed attachment role of being an emotional support for her mother. Cathy, however, seemed to stand back emotionally and hint at some criticism of her mother. When Mary responded to this with tears, Cathy eventually ceased any criticism and turned to reassure her mother (see Figure 7.3).

In some ways the relationship between the women paralleled the marital relationship, except that Mary appeared to be in the emotionally dependent role.

The relationship between Cathy and her father appeared more emotionally distant though again it did seem that possibly Cathy was more emotionally dominant and that her father turned to her for support rather than the reverse.

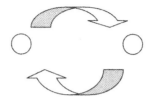

Cathy	Mother
Confident	Anxious
Critical . . .	Feels blame . . .
Offers reassurance	Seeks reassurance . . .

Figure 7.3 Cathy and her mother

Attachment system

It seemed, as was also exemplified by the quotes from Cathy in earlier chapters, that she was emotionally triangulated between her parents (see Figure 7.4).

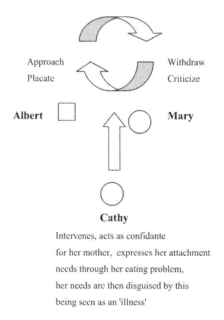

Figure 7.4 Family attachment system

She sensed her parents' unhappiness and was aware of the conflicts between them and this prompted her to intervene emotionally in their dynamics. She appeared to hold a significant role in taking care of their attachment needs, especially in relation to her mother. Cathy had also described how her parents became angry and could accuse each other if they perceived Cathy to be closer to one of them than the other.

Therapist–family attachment system

From an attachment perspective it seemed to us that it was very hard in this family for anyone to be emotionally looked after and comforted. In fact the person who was ostensibly the most vulnerable – Cathy – appeared to be in the role of meeting her parents' attachment needs rather than the reverse. It also seemed to us that since neither parent may have had experience of being comforted it might not be easy for them to trust us – the therapy team – to offer this. In fact it appeared that Cathy was the most able to trust us and gain support, though there was an element of her joining with us against her parents. She would indicate that she could understand our suggestions and agreed with us in adopting a psychologically minded approach. There also appeared to be the possible prospect of her being liberated from her role as an emotional carer for her parents. Consistent with this we felt that it might be helpful to offer some support for the parents and their marriage in order to help them with their own emotional processes. At the same time this could be a way of helping Cathy to help ease her out of the role as emotional carer for her parents.

Collaborative formulation

At the time that we conducted this work we had thought less about how we could share such formulations with a family. There are broadly three approaches we now take to this important issue. First, we share these ideas progressively, especially through a discussion of trans-generational patterns and repetitions across the generations. Second, we can have a discussion with family members about how we all, including the therapists, have different ways of handling our feelings and sources of support and comfort. Hence we can discuss some impressions we are forming about how the family members are able to turn to each other and also how difficult this can be in the context of the problem. Finally, we attempt to discuss our evolving relationship with the family, for example in terms of how we might be able to support each of them and how we might know if what we were offering was helpful or not.

Exploration of the problem

A focus of exploration for Cathy and her family was initially on how the anorexia had impacted on them all and their relationships. This draws from narrative approaches in attempting to map the influence of the problems on people and in turn mapping the influence that they can have on the problems. More specifically an ANT focus is to elaborate how the problems make each of them feel and how it influences how they feel about each other. In particular Mary described that she felt that she had failed as a mother and that it was her fault that Cathy had the problems. For her part Cathy described that she felt bad that she was causing everyone to feel worried and upset and wished they would not worry about her so much. Albert said that he felt helpless in that he just did not know what to do for the best to make anything better. This led into a discussion about comforting and how they had tried to offer each other reassurance and comfort each other. Albert said he had told his wife not to worry but this did not seem to help. Cathy said that, likewise, she reassured her mother that she would be alright and that it was not her mother's fault. In these discussions the focus on comforting seemed to be on Mary. Though from Cathy there was the classic paradox that at the same time as telling her mother not to worry she was also presenting her with a considerable amount to worry about in terms of her illness (see Figure 7.5).

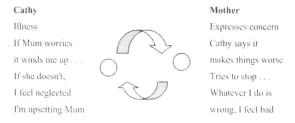

Cathy	Mother
Illness	Expresses concern
If Mum worries	Cathy says it
it winds me up . . .	makes things worse
If she doesn't,	Tries to stop . . .
I feel neglected	Whatever I do is
I'm upsetting Mum	wrong, I feel bad

Figure 7.5 Self-perpetuating cycle: 'I'm ill, but don't worry . . .'

We perceived this pattern as a self-perpetuating cycle of negative feelings since both of them end up feeling it is their fault and that they are to blame in various ways. We discussed this, and other patterns, in an attempt to encourage semantic understanding of their dynamics; we thought this might be especially relevant for Mary. More broadly it was to help her develop an understanding, not just of this pattern, but to encourage her to process events in terms of causal and temporal sequences as opposed to a predominantly emotional (preoccupied) way of responding. This did not appear to be easy for her to do and she appeared to regard thinking in this way as relatively peripheral to the problem. Such dismissing of cognition can be seen to be consistent with a preoccupied emotional orientation and hence we anticipate that some movement to a less emotionally focused way of thinking is a gradual process.

Key to this exploration is to make trans-generational connections. Focusing extensively on current family dynamics can convey a sense of blaming and often elicits some defensive responses. We therefore drew out a

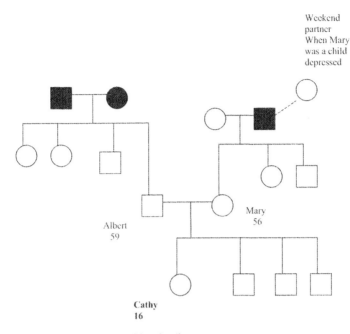

Figure 7.6 Genogram: Cathy and her family

family genogram (see Figure 7.6) and started with a discussion of whether there had been similar problems elsewhere in the family and then moved to an exploration of trans-generational patterns of attachment and comforting. To start with we asked Albert and Mary in turn about the attachment they had with each of their parents. In this we were careful to ask about both *semantic* memories – an overall cognitive description but also prompted them to offer *episodic* memories in terms of examples of events, activities and interactions with their parent that illustrated their overall semantic descriptions. We then asked for a description of the relationship between their parents – again inviting semantic and episodic memories. This was then followed by asking specifically about how they were comforted by each of their parents when they were hurt, ill or upset.

Mary described an unhappy childhood in which her mother had been emotionally distant and unavailable largely because her husband had a long-term affair with another woman. She remembered vividly seeing her mother upset as her husband got dressed up to go and see his other partner. She described how her mother had 'put up with a lot ... as people used to then'. Mary described quite close relations with her brother and sister but with some competition for their mother's limited time. However, she had no memories of being comforted and explained tearfully that she had 'never been ill', in effect that she had never been allowed to be. Albert painted a picture of his mother as someone who had been overweight, lethargic and who had played on her illnesses a lot to 'avoid her responsibilities'. By contrast his father had been a hard-working but 'angry man ... due to an enduring physical illness'. It was a picture of a man who was strict and at times frightening but after losing his temper would feel guilty and attempt to 'bribe' Albert with sweets. Family times, such as mealtimes, were not enjoyable and the relationship between his parents was distant and cold. His memory of being comforted when he was ill with chicken pox was of being placed in a bed with the other children so they all got, and got over, the illness in one go!

The following extracts are part of an interview with the family with a particular focus being directed on a consideration of their relationships to food, memories of mealtimes and the role of food as a form of comfort:

In the first extract the parents describe their memories of being comforted in their families:

RD:	Can you remember how you were comforted by either of your parents when you were ill or upset?
Mary:	I was never ill [tears welling up]
Albert:	My father had a very quick temper, he could fly ... like that ... but then he would come down even further than he was before he went up, and then he was full of remorse and he would generally give me money to go the pictures. Because where we were there were three local cinemas near where we lived and we used to have aniseed balls and a trip to the pictures.
RD:	And that's what he did if you were a bit ill, or upset ... Mary you can't remember?
Mary:	Never, never got ... anything
Albert:	You mean it didn't happen or you just can't remember?
Mary:	Didn't happen ... [crying]

We can see in this extract that neither of them had particularly good experiences of comfort. For Mary thinking back prompts painful memories of her mother being unavailable. Albert can recall some instances of being comforted, but these are associated with a volatile and frightening father.

The interview progressed to focus more specifically on the issue of comfort but also, given anorexia was the central presenting problem, with how this connected with food. The family was asked about patterns of comfort in the previous generation that the parents had experienced:

RD:	Some families talk about ... if they were hurt or as a child upset maybe they were given food as a comfort. Any examples of anything like that? ... Mary you were saying you were given clothes ... For example, when I was ill my mother always made me soup. I still make myself soup if I am ill ...
Mary:	I was never ill [tears starting to well up ... Starts to cry]
RD:	Chicken soup ...
Mary:	I don't remember being ill [crying quietly]
Albert:	I can always remember my mother and father had the philosophy that if one gets something they were all put together in one bed. So if one got chicken pox she used to put us all to bed together. So that we all had it, get it over with ...
RD:	Sorry Mary – can you carry on?
Mary:	Does now, we are very close now but we weren't then but then my Mum had her problems

Food, which is an important vehicle of comfort and can be a setting for family social occasions, was not remembered with any warm or pleasant memories. What was also striking was that for both Mary and Albert such memories were hard to access and when they were able eventually to do so these quickly evoked negative emotions. For both parents it appeared difficult to make connections between food and relationships, though interestingly this was quickly picked up by Cathy who was able to make a link between use of biscuits and an emotional relationship, albeit a negative one, of favouritism in Mary's eyes.

Cathy:	I thought Dad was the favourite so he got loads of sweets ...
Mary:	Dad? ... He always used to get chocolate biscuits
Cathy:	Cos he was the favourite, you told me ...
Mary:	Yes, he was his ma's favourite, you and Laura, you and Laura were regarded as the favourites, and the other two were ... which I found hard to realise but ...

These extracts help to illustrate some features of the stories that the parents held about their childhood experiences. From this we had a sense that neither of the parents had experienced being comforted as a child when they were hurt or upset. For Mary, powerful memories seemed to be evoked of her mother's unavailability and this left her with a wish for things to be different with her children but possibly little in the way of experience of how to do this. For Albert this seemed on the surface less painful, though his memories of his father are generally of a frightening and unpredictable man. In his conversation Albert seems to equate comfort with bribery and Mary does attempt to correct him to consider a softer view of giving the children treats.

An important component of the trans-generational interview is to move to an exploration of corrective and replicative scripts. For Mary one of her corrective scripts was not to put up with things as her mother had done, so not to suffer in silence. In describing this we started to wonder whether she was talking about her current marriage and whether she was unhappy and wanted to change things. Albert said that he also had hoped that his family life would be warmer than what he had experienced in his own family. In relation to Cathy and the other children both Mary and Albert said that they had hoped they could have a closer relationship with their children than they had each experienced. However, this seemed difficult for them. In particular Mary stated that though she had tried she felt she had failed and could not get it right:

RD:	Can I ask, connecting with that ... what ideas did that give you, maybe starting with you Mary what ideas did it give you about how you wanted to do it differently with your kids. Thinking back about how it was for you?
Mary:	I used to shout at mine a lot, maybe because I was shouted at a lot...

Cathy then appears to help her mother out by pointing out that she did try to keep one good part of her childhood experience alive in the current family through the Sunday roast dinners:

Cathy:	You continued the family roast thing for a while...
Mary:	Yeah ... we always had...
Cathy:	You'd have got that from your childhood wouldn't you...?
Albert:	Normal thing wasn't it...
Cathy:	And then that carried on when you had your kids

This pattern of Cathy coming to her mother's emotional rescue was a recurring one in the sessions. But it also seemed to be an ambivalent process in that Cathy would also engage in bouts of either explicitly or implicitly criticizing her mother and then comfort her, almost a form of emotional 'taunting'.

As the interview moved to considering Cathy's perceptions of the family meals and what she has learnt from these we can see both what scripts Cathy has acquired from her family and undertones of a process of implicit criticism of her mother:

> RD: Thinking of this as traditions weaving down the genera-
> tions, what traditions do you think you will continue …
> when you will have your family?
>
> Cathy: Not so much a tradition but I will want all my kids to sit and
> eat together and stuff, social event every single day. That's
> not what I picked up but it's what I want … we went
> through a stage of going for meals as a family with the boys
> and their girlfriends … I'd like to see that with my kids

Mary became very quiet as she listened to Cathy's ideals of how she would be with her own children in the future. Probably it was something that Mary had wanted but which seemed now to underline her sense of failure as a mother.

As this trans-generational interview moved from the questions about the relationships with each parent to an exploration of corrective and replicative scripts it was possible to see that neither Mary nor Albert appeared to have previously made conscious connections about these patterns. For Mary this was difficult and as in many of the sessions she seems trapped in the emotions of her childhood and a sense of failure over Cathy. Though Albert did make some connections these also appeared to be negative memories in terms of thinking about food and gifts for the children as being bribes. Cathy on the one hand offered some positive connections in emphasizing how she can see that her mother tried to keep the tradition of a Sunday roast meal going, however on the other hand, her conversation moved into some elements that she probably realized would be upsetting for her mother as she recounted how in the future she intends to have sociable mealtimes with her children. During this sequence her mother became very quiet, possibly absorbing this as a criticism of her.

Exploration of alternatives – and change

This stage focuses on attempts with the family and the individual members to consider changes in the attachment narratives and, intertwined with these, changes in the emotional processes within and between people. From the exploration stage we formulated a number of directions for interventions:

> 1 A trans-generational pattern of lack of secure attachments and
> lack of experiences of attachment for both parents. In narrative
> terms neither of them appeared to have developed coherent
> stories of attachments, expression of needs, patterns of com-
> forting or ideas about the potential value of openness in com-
> municating about their feelings and needs.

> 2 The parents appeared to have a painful and emotionally unsa-
> tisfying relationship and one in which they were unable to meet
> each other's attachment needs.
> 3 Cathy appeared to be triangulated into her parents' relationship.
> She was aware of the negative impact their relationship had on
> her and it appeared that her parents had some awareness of this
> but were so emotionally reactive that they were rarely able to
> think abut this in a constructive way.

Enhancing coherent narrative regarding attachment (stage 1)

This was initiated by the discussions of trans-generational attachment patterns. It was continued in the sessions by reference to these patterns and helping to make connections with current processes. Development of coherence is also fostered by *reflecting team discussion* which allow different, multiple descriptions to be offered regarding their emotional processes. For example, the reflecting teams and the discussions with the therapist focused on the positive intentions of both parents in the ways that they were attempting to do things differently for Cathy, given the difficult experiences that they had both experienced. To take one example, we discussed how Mary going to work could be seen as her attempting to show her daughter a model of an independent woman who was not going to be trapped and dependent, as the grandmothers on both sides of the family had been. Albert too had tried to be a different kind of father who did not shout at his children and had been very close to Cathy when she was younger.

The narrative approach of exploring unique outcomes adds to the development of alternative narratives by focusing on exceptions and times that their relationships were different, for example how they managed things before Cathy became ill. Cathy, for example, had described how she liked it when her mother had time with her when she was not working. The significance of this time and the possibility of them having some more time together was discussed. Cathy had also enjoyed going with her parents for family meals with her brothers and their girlfriends. The differences that being in other social settings and family groupings could make to the experience of and freedom from the eating problems was discussed. Likewise, the linking of food and feelings developed in stage 2 was expanded with broader discussions about the links between emotions, appetite, comfort and food.

Exploration of the marital relationship (stage 2)

By working with the couple we both implicitly and explicitly encouraged the development of relational narratives that connected Cathy's feelings, eating and appetite with family emotional processes and conflicts. We engaged in three sessions which were dedicated to work with the parents as a couple. We framed this in terms of the impact of anorexia on them and their right to have a break: 'A difficulty such as anorexia coming into your lives can become very draining and leave you little chance to talk about your own relationship and concerns. It may also be that some things are easier and more appropriate to talk about with just the two of you and not involving Cathy'. This was an attempt to ease the triangulation process in which Cathy appeared to be involved. For some parents even this kind of suggestion can be too threatening, and so sometimes we emphasize that probably most of what they talk about will be the problems that they are having with 'the anorexia' but that they deserve at least some space for their own needs. We would also add that all parents, especially having been through such difficulties, need a chance to 'recharge their batteries' or they will be less able to help their child resist the problems.

For Mary and Albert their own problems were quite near the surface. Mary had several times alluded to no longer being prepared to 'put up with things'. In the first of the sessions as a couple Mary rapidly stated that she was very unhappy in the marriage and that she wanted to leave Albert. She went on to describe having had a brief affair some years ago and that later she found out that Albert had done so as well. She connected her feelings to her own mother's situation and this left her with a strong sense of not wanting to 'put up' with things and suffer in silence, as her mother had done. This seemed like a spectre that hung over her – a fear that she would end up unhappy and alone like her mother. The session appeared to become difficult for Mary and she retreated to a position of hurt and rejection of Albert. We invited them to try an approach in the session which we have come to describe as '*structured reflective conversation*'. This consisted of two sets of conversations. Mary had a conversation with a female therapist while Albert and I listened, followed by a conversation between me and Albert while Mary and my female colleague listened. The conversation picked up the themes for the trans-generational attachment interview but specifically focused on the couple's relationship in terms of how it was different or similar to their parents' relationship. Also, it focused on corrective and replicative scripts in terms of how they hoped their marriage would be similar or different. The conversation also included the nature of their emotional connections and allowed each partner to discuss positive and negative aspects of their relationship. We also asked about how the relationship was at the start in terms of their corrective and replicative script regarding their parents' marriages, and then at what point they feel their own relationship significantly changed. This connects with the idea of '*attachment injuries*' or turning points where things may have deteriorated.

As with many couples in this interview they both stated that initially they had hoped it would be different from their parents' relationships by being close, affectionate and warm. However, it transpired that intimacy had become very problematic with a common pattern of pursuit avoidance having evolved in their relationship. This had been triggered by Albert experiencing hurt and insecurity on discovering that Mary had had an intimate relationship previous to her involvement with him. Even though it had happened in the past, because Mary had not told him about it, it had been experienced as a deep hurt and betrayal. Mary was able to express to the female therapist how painful and abusive the pattern of their relationship had become for her. For his part, Albert was shocked to realize how his demands were experienced by Mary as being extremely aversive. He was able to ask Mary to forgive him and Mary stated that this helped but she was not sure if it was too late. However, what appeared to be the genuine recognition of each other's feelings and distress did seem to us to be quite a significant moment in our work with them. The structure of each being assisted in talking with another therapist as well as being assisted in their listening by a therapist of the same sex appeared to help this process. We were also able to validate these efforts as being courageous on their part and as not only helpful for themselves but for Cathy, and we contemplated with them whether Cathy had noticed some of their sadness and distress.

A danger in such moments can be that as each partner makes their attachment needs visible and, as in Albert's case, attempts to express remorse, there is also a potential for further hurt. Mary's statement that it might have been too late could potentially have felt like a rejection in the face of his remorse and tears. However, we discussed with them that for many couples the sort of changes they were making were very hard and typically took time before trust would come back. We suggested that it would take time for Mary to believe that Albert would not make angry demands, and for Albert that Mary would not threaten to leave and dismiss him. Individual sessions can be helpfully interspersed with the couple's sessions. Albert attended an individual session with us and was able to reflect on how shocked he had been on recognizing how Mary had felt over the years. It also allowed him to discuss how important Cathy had been in their intimacy. Specifically, their physical intimacy had been warmest when Cathy was born and Mary had been very happy for several years. This confirmed the picture of Cathy's entanglement with her parents and how special she had been from the moment of her birth.

Discussion of child's entanglement in parents' relationship (stage 3)

In family sessions, individual sessions and also in a number of sessions with Cathy and one of her parents, we addressed the central issues of Cathy's emotional entaglement in the couple relationship. We worked with both parents to create more understanding about their relationship needs. We also explored Cathy's role by looking at Mary's role as carer of her own mother.

Mary's mother had been a sad, depressed woman who, though angry with Mary, had nevertheless depended on her. Mary had described that she too had been angry with her children and disappointed that they had not acknowledged what she had tried to provide for them. She was able to admit that she needed affection from Cathy. We also discussed that Cathy had been, and still was, influenced by their relationship and talked about how they too, as all children are, had been upset to see their parents' unhappiness. However, Mary and Albert held the belief that Cathy was not really influenced by their conflicts, or that these could not have 'caused' her problems. In a session with her father Cathy was able to explain that she was upset by the conflicts between her parents and felt pressure to intervene. Likewise, Cathy was able to explain this to her mother and also that she did not blame her, but did want to see her being happier. We sympathized with their struggles and added that blaming themselves and each other was not helpful and that there was no simple explanation for Cathy's illness. Mary continually repeated that she felt that perhaps it would be better for Cathy if she and Albert split up. We discussed this with both parents, especially encouraging consideration of what the possible consequences of this might be in terms of how it might lead Cathy to feel.

Integration and maintaining contact (stage 4)

The aim of the discussion in the previous stage increasingly moves towards encouraging family members to be able to integrate their experiences and build more coherent narratives. This integration is continuous but the reflecting team can help model this process as our discussions move towards possible integrative themes. Also reflecting team input helps to elaborate the types of information that they are able to process about feelings and relationships. It can also support or offer a 'scaffolding' of their abilities to generate more coherent narratives. An important part of this is to return to integrative processes in terms of what they had learnt from their early experiences and then to make connections with the learning that may be going on in our sessions.

For attachment theory, loss, abandonment, rejection as opposed to continuity and trust, are important themes. The ending of therapy therefore importantly connects with integrative themes about what people have learnt from their life experiences, specifically also with reflections on what has been helpful or otherwise from the sessions with us. Despite many warm and supportive words, the ending of therapy can serve to reinforce deeply held attachment narratives that you cannot trust people or what they say and just like everyone else therapists do not really care, it was all a sham and that you end up being abandoned.

This was very nearly the scenario that presented itself at the end of our work with Cathy. Since she was about to go to university and the situation had improved substantially, just about all aspects of her professional support system was withdrawing at the same time. Our team too had overlooked some signals from Cathy about how difficult this might be. For example, she repeatedly said how attached she was to the psychologist with whom she had been working and as the time for her to leave for university grew closer she repeated how she would miss her. Somewhat oblivious to this, partly due to the usual pressures of waiting lists and demands from other families, we too were intending to end our work with Cathy and her family. For the last session they attended politely and thanked us profusely for our efforts with them. However, as the end approached it became starkly clear that Cathy was becoming very distressed though bravely trying to fight this. It was also clear that we were the last of the remaining support still in place. We also became acutely aware that this was the first time Cathy had shown distress with us. For this vulnerable young woman who had been emotionally propping up her parents but now had no prospect of support herself, this was now too much to bear. Ironically this was the point at which her parents had resolved some of their problems. For example, they had planned a holiday together and Mary had said that she was planning to work on her relationship with Albert and was seeing it more positively.

However, though these changes had been of benefit to Cathy she was also going to be faced with separation from her parents by going away to university in another city. Consequently, we discussed with them whether ending in this way was appropriate or not. This elicited some important conversations about support, emotional needs and being able to turn to people for help when they needed to. We together decided that instead of ending that day we would continue to see them when Cathy came back from university at two-monthly intervals and also that we would phone her and make contact with the person the college had arranged to give Cathy professional support. We finally offered to see her parents in the meanwhile if they found this helpful.

Cathy's case was a turning point for us in helping us to see the importance of offering continuity of support. In many cases this does not need to be frequent contact but can be an important symbol of continuing care and attachment. In the event they only came once more as a family and we had telephone contact with Cathy a few times. However, we are very sure that she would have deteriorated dramatically without this.

Arguably the issues here are not simply or predominantly about whether attachment dependencies have been created. The ending in itself is a powerful narrative about the nature of attachments. We also discussed with the family that there would be ups and downs and there would be future struggles and considered what these might be and how they could support each other and Cathy. Such discussion of relapse can be seen in attachment terms as helping families towards a more coherent and less dismissive narrative about attachments. Otherwise we run the risk of colluding with dismissive narratives that ignore that the future will invariably hold difficulties, especially as Cathy was leaving home. By developing some realistic plans for how to manage future needs and problems it also offers a more coherent narrative, avoiding a preoccupied narrative that becomes inordinately fearful and emotionally saturated and that prevents the development of plans for dealing with feelings in the future. Again there is a delicate balance. Sometimes as therapists we can become overly fearful of letting go, and in communicating that we are worried we do not help the family to contain and manage the anxiety of a transition.

Formats for exploration

Exploring patterns of comforting

The following questions can be employed in work with individuals, couples or families:

> - When you were upset or frightened as a child what happened?
> - How did you get to feel better? Who helped you to feel better? How did they do this?
> - What have you learnt from this for your own family?
> - What do you want to do the same?
> - What do you want to do differently?
> - How do people comfort each other in your own family/relationship?
> - How do you comfort your children?
> - How do they comfort you?

In the case of couples the conversation is with one person while the other listens. For some people remembering the incidents discussed can be difficult and they may need reassurance. In some cases the questions may need to become more hypothetical, for example – What do you imagine happened? What would you have liked to happen? How do you think you might have felt if you had been comforted, held, supported and so on. The questions move to integrative ones in terms of what has been learnt from the experiences, what sense has been made of the events and also to the present in terms of the relevance of the experiences to current relationships.

With younger children the exploration can include use of drawing, toys and puppets to demonstrate how comfort was or could have been given.

Exploring attachment narratives through the family genogram

Exploring the parents' attachments

Draw up a family genogram with the family. This can be conducted with the children present and asked to listen. At times the children may also be invited to comment or answer questions.

The emotional atmosphere in the parent's family

- How would you describe the emotional atmosphere in your family – cold, warm, distant?
- How physical was your family? Do you remember lots of hugs and kisses or was there little touching?
- How was distress, pain, sadness dealt with?

Exploring the nature of the parents' attachments to their own parents

- How would you describe your relationship with your mother/father?
- Who were you closest to, your mother or your father?
- Did your closeness change as you grew older?
- Can you give some examples of being close or distant?

The relationship between the grandparents

Questions about the grandparents' relationship can bring out stories about the parents' childhood experiences and prompt a consideration of how their own children experience their relationship.

- How would you describe your parents' (the grandparents) relationship – cold, warm, distant, passionate, conflicts?
- What differences do you see between the relationships between the maternal grandparents vs. the paternal grandparents?
- In what ways are either of the grandparents' relationships similar to your own?

Corrective and replicative scripts

- What have you tried to make similar or different to either of these relationships?
- What do you value vs. feel critical about in either of your parents' relationships?

Influence on the parents' relationship with their own children

These are questions which invite the parents to consider how their own experiences have consciously or unconsciously influenced and shaped their relationships with their children.

- How do you see your relationship [mother and father in turn] with your children?
- How are you different with your children to how your parents were with you?
- Do you think you are closer or more distant to your children than your parents were with you?

Following the interview with the parents, the children can be asked to comment on what they understand from it, how it makes sense of how their parents are with each other and them, whether they have heard anything new in the interview.

Structured reflective conversation

The aim of this is to help family members or a couple to be able to listen to each other without interruptions or patterns of accusation, counter-accusation and blaming. For a couple there are two therapists in the room. One therapist sits with each of the couples, usually in a same sex pairing, though there can be variations on this. One therapist has a conversation with one partner. The conversation can, for example, be structured as a trans-generational interview, exploring patterns of comfort or instances of attachment breakdown or injury. Following a conversation, usually taking between 5 and 15 minutes, the other therapist and partner have a conversation on the same theme. Following this each partner reflects with the help of their therapist on what they have heard. Finally, there is an open discussion on what has been triggered by the conversations.

Variations can be carried out in therapy with families, for example parents as being one group and children as another, gender groupings and so on.

To summarize then:

- Family or couple paired with co-therapist each
- Discuss with the family the potential value of a reflective conversation
- Two sets of conversation: group A talks – B listens; Group B talks – A listens
- Reflective conversation across the two groups

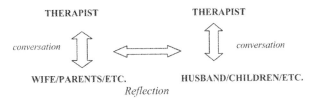

THERAPIST   THERAPIST

conversation   *conversation*

WIFE/PARENTS/ETC.   HUSBAND/CHILDREN/ETC.

Reflection

Reflecting team discussion: attachment narratives

These have the usual format of reflecting teams as outlined by Tom Anderson (1987) and others. However, they have the added focus of picking up on attachment themes and emotional processes in the family. This can include questions and reflections regarding current attachment processes, trans-generational patterns, patterns of comforting, attachment disruptions and 'injuries', future-oriented conversations about how attachments may evolve and change in the future, and integrative conversations. A few examples of the kinds of questions and conversations that this might trigger are:

- I wonder how the parents feel they have been able to do things differently the same as their parents did? What have they discovered from thinking abut this? Has it helped them to think, act, feel differently?
- If they were able to change how they comfort each other, what changes would they make? What could help this to happen? How might this change in the future?
- How does the family feel about this therapy situation? How has this changed from previous feelings? What helps them to be able to trust us and what gets in the way of that?
- What have they discovered about their attachments patterns in the past? Do they think history needs to repeat itself? What could help to alter history repeating itself?
- Looking back over the events in the past how do they think it has made them the family that they are?
- In what ways will the children do things differently in the future? Do they want their family, when and if they have one, to be more cuddly? Or do they want to be more independent and self-sufficient?

References

Ainsworth, M.D.S. (1973) The development of infant–mother attachment, in B.M. Caldwell and H. Riccuiti (eds) *Review of Child Development Research*, Vol. 3. Chicago: Chicago University Press.

Ainsworth, M.D.S. and Bell, S.M. (1970) Attachment, exploration, and separation. Illustrated by the behaviour of one-year olds in the strange situation, *Child Development*, 41: 49–67.

Ainsworth, M.D., Blehar, M.C., Waters, E. and Wall, S. (1978) *Patterns of Attachment: A Psychological Study of the Strange Situation*. Hillside, NK: Lawrence Erlbaum.

Andersen, T. (1987) The reflecting team: dialogue and meta-dialogue in clinical work, *Family Process*, 26: 415–28.

Anderson, H., Goolishan, H.A. and Windermand, L. (1986) Problem determined systems: toward transformation in family therapy, *Journal of Strategic and Systemic Therapies*, 5: 1–13.

Baerger, D.R. and McAdams, D. (1999) Life story coherence and its relation to psychological well-being, *Narrative Inquiry*, 9: 69–96.

Bales, R.F. (1950) *Interaction Process Analysis: A Method for the Study of Small Groups*. Cambridge, MA: Addison-Wesley.

Baron-Cohen, S., Tager-Flusberg, H. and Cohen, D.J. (eds) (1993) *Understanding Other Minds*. Oxford: Oxford University Press.

Bartholomew, K. and Horowitz, L.M. (1991) Attachment styles among young adults: a test of a four-category model, *Journal of Personality and Social Psychology*, 61(2): 226–44.

Bateson, G. (1972) *Steps to an Ecology of Mind*. New York: Ballantine.

Belsky, J. (1999) Interactional and contextual determinants of attachment security, in J. Cassidy and P.R. Shaver (eds) *Handbook of Attachment*. New York: Guilford Press.

Bion, W.R. (1962) *Learning from Experience*. London: Heinemann.

Bordin, E. (1979) The generalizability of the psychoanalytic concept of the working alliance, *Psychotherapy, Theory, Research and Practice*, 16: 252–60.

Bowlby, J. (1969) Attachment, *Attachment and Loss*, Vol. 1. New York: Basic Books.

Bowlby, J. (1973) *Attachment and Loss*, Vols 1 and 2. New York: Basic Books.

Bowlby, J. (1980) Loss, *Attachment and Loss*, Vol. 3. New York: Basic Books.

Bowlby, J. (1988) *A Secure Base*. New York: Basic Books.

Brennan, K.A. and Shaver, P.R. (1995) Dimensions of adult attachment, affect regulation, and romantic relationship functioning, *Personality and Social Psychology Bulletin*, 21(3): 267–83.

Bretherton, I. (1985) Attachment theory: retrospect and prospect, in I. Bretherton and E. Waters (eds) *Growing Points of Attachment Theory and Research* (Monographs for the Society for Research in Child Development), 50 (1–2, Serial No. 209): 3–35.

Bretherton, I. (1995) A communicational perspective on attachment relations and internal working models, in E. Waters, B.E. Vaughn, G. Posada and K. Kondo-Ikemura (eds) *Caregiving, Cultural, and Cognitive Perspectives on Secure-base Behaviour and Working Models: New Growing Points of Attachment Theory and Research.* (Monographs of the Society for Research in Child Development.) 60 (2–3, Serial no. 244).

Brown, G.W. and Harris, T. (1989) *The Social Origins of Depression.* London: Routledge.

Bruner, J. (1990) *Acts of Meaning.* Cambridge, MA: Harvard University Press.

Byng-Hall, J. (1980) The symptom bearer as marital distance regulator: clinical implications, *Family Process*, 19: 355–65.

Byng-Hall, J. (1995) *Rewriting Family Scripts.* London: Guilford Press.

Cain, A.C. and Fast, I. (1972) Children's disturbed reactions to parent suicide, in A.C. Cain (ed.) *Survivors of Suicide.* Springfield, Ill: C.C. Thomas.

Cassidy, J., Woodhouse, S.S, Cooper, G., Hoffman, K., Powell, B & Rodenberg, M. (2005) Examination of the Precursors of Infant Attachment Security In L.J. Berlin, Y. Ziv, L. Amaya-Jackson & M.T. Greenberg (eds). Enhancing Early Attachment. Basingstoke: Taylor-Francis.

Catlin, G. and Epstein, S. (1992) Unforgettable experiences: the relation of basic beliefs to extreme life events and childhood relationships with parents, *Social Cognition*, 10: 189–209.

Cecchin, G. (1987) Hypothesizing, circularity and neutrality revisited: an invitation to curiosity, *Family Process*, 26(4): 405–13.

Coulehan, R., Friedlander, M.L. and Heatherington, L. (1998) Transforming narratives: a change event in constructivist family therapy, *Family Process*, 37: 17–33.

Craik, K. (1943) *The Nature of Explanation.* Cambridge: Cambridge University Press.

Crittenden, P.M. (1995) Attachment and psychopathology, in S. Goldberg, R. Muir and J. Kerr (eds) *John Bowlby's Attachment Theory: Historical, Clinical and Social Significance.* New York: The Analytic Press.

Crittenden, P. (1997) Truth, error, omission, distortion, and deception: an application of attachment theory to the assessment and treatment of psychological disorder, in S.M. Clany Dollinger and L.F. DiLalla (eds) *Assessment and Intervention Issues Across the Life Span.* London: Lawrence Erlbaum.

Crittenden, P.M. (2004) Workshop on Dynamic Maturational Model and personal communication, Reading, UK.

Dallos, R. (1991) *Family Belief Systems, Therapy and Change*. Buckingham: Open University Press.

Dallos, R. (2000) *An Introduction to Family Therapy*. Buckingham: Open University Press.

Dallos, R. (2004) Attachment narrative therapy: integrating ideas from narrative and attachment theory in systemic family therapy with eating disorders, *Journal of Family Therapy*, 26(1): 40–66.

Dallos, S. and Dallos, R. (1997) *Couples, Sex and Power: The Politics of Desire*. Buckingham: Open University Press.

Dallos, R. and Draper, R. (2005) *An Introduction to Family Therapy*, 2nd edn. Maidenhead: Open University Press/McGraw-Hill.

Dallos, R. and Hamilton-Brown, L. (2000) Pathways to problems – an exploratory study of how problems evolve vs dissolve in families, *Journal of Family Therapy*, 22: 375–93.

Davies, P.T. and Cummings, E.M. (1998) Exploring children's emotional security as a mediator of the link between marital relations and child adjustment, *Child Development*, 69: 124–39.

De Shazer, S. (1982) *Patterns of Brief Therapy: An Ecosystemic Approach*. New York: Guilford Press.

Diamond, G. S. and Siqueland, L. (1998) Emotions, attachments and the relational reframe, *Journal of Structural and Strategic Therapy*, 17: 36–50.

Doane, J.A. and Diamond, D. (1994) *Affect and Attachment in the Family*. New York: Basic Books.

Donaldson, M. (1978) *Children's Minds*. New York: Norton Ekman.

Epstein, S. (1973) The self concept revisited or a theory of a theory, *American Psychologist*, 28: 404–16.

Epstein, S. (1980) The self concept: a review and the proposal of an integrated theory of personality, in E. Strubb (ed.) *Basic Aspects and Current Research*. Englewood Cliffs, NJ: Prentice-Hall.

Eron, J.B. and Lund, T.W. (1993) How problems evolve and dissolve: integrating narrative and strategic concepts, *Family Process*, 32: 291–309.

Feeney, J. (2003) The systemic nature of couple relationships: an attachment perspective, in P. Erdman and T. Caffery (eds) *Attachment and Family Systems*. Hove: Brunner-Routledge.

Fonagy, P., Steele, H., Moran, G.S., Steele, M. and Higgit, A. (1991a) The capacity for understanding mental states: the reflective self in parent and child and its significance for security of attachment, *Infant Mental Health Journal*, 13: 200–17.

Fonagy, P., Steele, M. and Steele, H. (1991b) Maternal representations of attachment during pregnancy predicts the organisation of infant–mother attachment at one year of age, *Child Development*, 62: 880–93.

Fonagy, P., Leigh, T., Steele, M. et al. (1996) The relation of attachment status, psychiatric classification, and response to psychotherapy, *Journal of Counselling and Clinical Psychology*, 64(1): 22–31.

Foreman, S. (1995) Inequalities of power, strategies of influence and sexual problems in couples. Unpublished PhD thesis. Milton Keynes: The Open University.

Foreman, S. and Dallos, R. (1992) Inequalities of power and sexual problems, *Journal of Family Therapy*, 14: 349–71.

Foucault, M. (1967) *Madness and Civilisation*. London: Tavistock.

Foucault, M. (1975) *The Archeology of Knowledge*. London: Tavistock.

Freud, S. (1922) *Introductory Lectures on Psycho-Analysis*. London: Allen and Unwin.

Freud, S. (1961) The ego and the id, in J. Strachey (ed. and trans.) *The Standard Edition of the Complete Works of Sigmund Freud*, Vol. 19. London: Hogarth Press.

George, C. and Salomon, J. (1999) Attachment and caregiving: the caregiving behavioural System, in J. Cassidy and P.R. Shaver (eds) *Handbook of Attachment: Theory, Research, and Clinical Applications*. New York: Guilford Press.

George, C., Kaplan, N. and Main, M. (1985) The Berkeley adult attachment interview. Unpublished. Berkeley, CA: Protocol Department of Psychology, University of California.

Gergen, K. (1999) *An Invitation to Social Constructionism*. London: Sage.

Gergen, K.J. and Davis, K.E. (eds) (1985) *The Social Construction of the Person*. New York: Springer-Verlag.

Goffman, E. (1959) *The Presentation of Self in Everyday Life*. Penguin: London.

Gottman, J.M. (1979) *Marital Interaction: Experimental Investigation*. New York: Academic Press.

Gottman, J.M. (1982) Emotional responsiveness in marital conversation, *Journal of Marriage and the Family*, 32: 108–20.

Habermas, T. and Bluck, S. (2000) Getting a life: the emergence of the life story in adolescence, *Psychological Bulletin*, 126(5): 748–69.

Haley, J. (1963) *Strategies of Psychotherapy*. New York: Grune and Stratton.

Haley, J. (1976) Development of a theory: a history of a research project, in C.E. Sluzki and D.C. Ransom (eds) *Double Bind: The Foundation of the Communicational Approach to the Family*. New York: Grune and Stratton.

Haley, J. (1987) *Problem Solving Therapy*, 2nd edn. San Fransisco, CA: Jossey-Bass.

Harvey, J.H., Orbuch, T.L. and Weber, A.L. (eds) (1992) *Attributions, Accounts and Close Relationships*. London: Springer-Verlag.

Hazan, C. and Shaver, P. (1987) Romantic love conceptualised as an attachment process, *Journal of Personality and Social Psychology*, 52: 511–24.

Hoffman, L. (1981) *Foundations of Family Therapy*. New York: Basic Books.

Hollway, W. (1989) *Subjectivity and Method in Psychology*. London: Sage.

Hollway, W. and Jefferson, T. (2001) Free association, narrative analysis and the defended subject: the case of Ivy, *Narrative Inquiry*, 11(1): 103–22.

Howes, C. (1999) Attachment relationships in the context of multiple caregivers, in J. Cassidy and P.R. Shaver (eds) *Handbook of Attachment*. New York: Guilford Press.

Jackson, D. (1957) The question of family homeostasis, *Psychiatry Quarterly Supplement*, 31: 79–99.

Jackson, D. (1965) The study of the family, *Family Process*, 4: 1–20.

Johnson, M. and Best, M. (2003) A systemic approach to restructuring adult attachment: the EFT model of couples therapy, in P. Erdman and T. Caffrey (eds) *Attachment and Family Systems*. New York: Brunner-Routledge.

Johnstone, L. and Dallos, R. (2006) *Formulation in Clinical Psychology and Counselling*. London: Brunner-Routledge.

Katz, L.F. and Gottman, J.M. (1996) Spillover effects of marital conflict: in search of parenting and coparenting mechanisms, in J.P. McHale and P. Cowan (eds) *New Directions in Child Development*, Vol. 74. San Fransisco: Jossey-Bass.

Kelly, G.A. (1955) *The Psychology of Personal Constructs*, Vols. 1 and 2. New York: Norton.

Kobak, R. (1999) The emotional dynamics of disruptions in attachment relationships: implications for theory, research, and clinical applications, in J. Cassidy and P.R. Shaver (eds) *Handbook of Attachment*. London: Guilford Press.

Kobak, R. and Cole, H. (1994) Attachment and meta-monitoring: implications for adolescent autonomy and psychopathology, in D. Cichetti and S.C. Toth (eds) *Disorders and Dysfunctions of the Self*. Based on Papers presented at the 5th Annual Rochester Symposium on Developmental Psychopathology, Vol. 5. Rochester, NY: University of Rochester Press.

Kohut, H. (1977) *The Restoration of the Self*. New York: Internatioal Universities Press.

Labov, W. (1972) *Language in the Inner City*. Philadelphia: University of Pennsylvania Press.

Labov, W. and Walesky, J. (1967) Narrative analysis: oral versions of personal experience, in J. Helm (ed.) *Essays on the Verbal and Visual Arts*. Seattle: University of Washington Press.

Laing, R.D. (1966) *The Politics of the Family and Other Essays*. London: Tavistock.

Lamb, M.E. (1977) The development of infant–mother and infant–father attachments in the second year of life, *Developmental Psychology*, 5: 355–7.

Leiper, R. (2001) *Working Through Setbacks in Psychotherapy*. London: Sage.

Luborsky, L., Critis-Cristoph, P., Leslie-Alexander, M.S., Margolis, M. and Cohen, M. (1983) Two helping alliance methods for predicting outcome of psychotherapy, *Journal of Nervous and Mental Disease*, 171(8): 480–91.

McCabe, A. and Peterson, C. (1991) Getting the story: a longitudinal study of parenting styles in eliciting narratives and developing narrative skill, in A. McCabe and C. Peterson (eds) *Developing Narrative Structure*. London: Lawrence Erlbaum.

McConnell, M. and Kerig, P. (1999) Inside the family circle: the relationship between coparenting and child adjustment in two-parent families. Paper presented at the Society for Research in Child Development, Albuquerque, NM, April.

Main, M. (1991) Meta-cognitive knowledge, metacognitive monitoring, and singular (coherent) vs Multiple (incoherent) models of attachment: findings and directions for future research, in P. Harris, J. Stevenson-Hinde and C. Parkes (eds) *Attachment Across the Lifecycle*. New York: Routledge-Kegan Paul.

Main, M. and Goldwyn, R. (1991) Adult attachment classification system, version 5. Unpublished manuscript, University of California, Berkeley, CA.

Main, M. and Solomon, J. (1986) Discovery of an insecure disorganised attachment pattern: procedures, findings and implications for the classification of behaviour, in M. Yogman and T.R. Brazelton (eds) *Affective Development in Infancy*. Norwood, NJ: Ablex.

Main, M. and Weston, D. R. (1981) The quality of the toddler's relationship to mother and father: related to conflict behaviour and readiness to establish new relationships, *Child Development*, 52: 932–40.

Main, M., Kaplan, N. and Cassidy, J. (1985) Security in infancy, childhood and adulthood: a move to the level of representation, in I. Bretherton and E. Waters (eds) *Growing Points of Attachment Theory and Research* (Monographs of the Society for Research in Child Development), 50(1–2, Serial No. 209).

Marx, K. and Engels, F. ([1846] 1970) *The German Ideology*. New York: International Publishers.

Mead, G.H. (1934) *Mind, Self and Society*. Chicago: Chicago University Press.

Mikulincer, M. and Shefi, E. (2000) Adult attachment style and cognitive reactions to positive affect: a test of mental cetagorization and creative problem solving, *Motivation and Emotion*, 24: 149–74.

Mikulincer, M., Shaver, P.R. and Pereg, D. (2003) Attachment theory and affect regulation: the dynamic, development, and cognitive consequences of attachment related strategies, *Motivation and Emotion*, 27(2): 77–102.

Minuchin, S., Rosman, B. and Baker, L. (1978) *Psychosomatic Families: Anorexia*. Cambridge, MA: Harvard University Press.

O'Hanlon, B. (1994) The third wave, *Family Therapy Networker*, 18: 18–29.

O'Hanlon, B. and Weiner-Davis, M. (1989) *In Search of Solutions*. New York: Norton.

Oppenheim, D. and Waters, H.S. (1985) Narrative processes and attachment representations: issues of development and assessment, in I. Bretherton and E. Waters (eds) *Growing Points of Attachment Theory and Research* (Monographs of the Society for Research in Child Development), 50(1–2, Serial No. 209): 197–215.

Owens, G., Croswell, J.A., Pan, H. et al. (1995) The prototype hypothesis and the origins of attachment working models: adult relationships with parents and romantic partners, in E. Waters, B.E. Vaughn, G. Posada and K. Kondo-Ikemura (eds) *Caregiving, Cultural, and Cognitive Perspectives on Secure-base Behaviour and Working Models: New Growing Points of Attachment Theory and Research* (Monographs of the Society for Research in Child Development), 60(2–3, Serial No. 244).

Palazzoli, M.S., Cecchin, G., Prata, G. and Boscolo, L. (1978) *Paradox and Counter Paradox*. New York: Jason Aronson.

Pereg, D. (2001) Mood and cognition: the moderating role of attachment style. Unpublished PhD dissertation. Bar-Ilan University, Israel.

Peterson, C. and McCabe, A. (1992) Parental styles of narrative elicitation: effect on children's narrative stricture and content, *First Language*, 12: 299–321.

Piaget, J. (1955) *The Child's Construction of Reality*. London: Routledge and Kegan Paul.

Pistole, M.C. (1994) Adult attachment styles: some thought on closeness-distance struggles, *Family Process*, 33: 147–59.

Potter, J. and Wetherell, M. (1987) *Discourse Social Psychology: Beyond Attitudes and Behaviour*. London: Sage.

Reiss, D. (1980) *The Family's Construction of Reality*. London: RKD.

Procter, H. (1981) Family construct psychology, in S. Walrond-Skinner (ed.) *Family Therapy and Approaches*. London: RKP.

Rogers, C. (1955) *Client-centred Therapy*. New York: Haughton Mifflin.

Salomon, J. and George, C. (1999) The measurement of attachment security in infancy and childhood, in J. Cassidy and P.R. Shaver (eds) *Handbook of Attachment: Theory, Research, and Clinical Applications*. New York: Guilford Press.

Schank, R.C. (1982) *Dynamic Memory: A Theory of Reminding and Learning in Computers and People*. Cambridge: Cambridge University Press.

Schank, R.C. and Abelson, R.P. (1977) *Scripts, Plans, Goals and Understanding*. Hillsdale, NJ: Erlbaum.

Shaver, P.R. and Mikulincer, M. (2002) Attachment related psychodynamics, *Attachment and Human Development*, 4: 133–61.

Simpson, J.A. and Gangestad, S.W. (1991) Individual differences in sociosexuality. Evidence for convergent and discriminant validity, *Journal of Personality and Social Psychology*, 60: 870–83.

Sluzki, C.E. (1992) Transformations: a blueprint for narrative changes in therapy, *Family Process*, 31: 217–30.

Steele, H. and Fonagy, P. (1995) Associations amongst attachment classifications of mothers, fathers and their infants, *Child Development*, 57: 571–5.

Stern, D. (1985) *The Interpersonal World of the Infant*. New York: Basic Books.

Talbot, J. and McHale (2003) Family level emotional climate and its impact on the flexibility of relationship representation, in P. Erdman and T. Caffery (eds) *Attachment and Family Systems*. Hove: Brunner-Routledge.

Tomm, K. (1984) One perspective on the Milan systemic approach: part 1, overview of development, theory and practice, *Journal of Marital and Family Therapy*, 2: 113–25.

Tomm, K. (1988) Interventive interviewing: part 3. Intending to ask circular, strategic or reflexive questions, *Family Process*, 27(1): 1–17.

Trevarthen, C. (1980) The foundations of intersubjectivity: development of interpersonal and cooperative understanding, in. D. Olson (ed.) *Essays in Honour of J.S. Bruner*. New York: W.W. Norton.

Trevarthen, C. (1992) The function of emotions in early infant communication and development, in J. Nadel and L. Camioni (eds) *New Perspectives in Early Communicative Development*. London: Routledge.

Trevarthen, C. and Aitkken, J. (2001) Infant intersubjectivity: research, theory and clinical applications, *Journal of Child Psychology and Psychiatry*, 42: 3–48.

Tulving, E. (1972) Episodic and semantic memory, in E. Tulving and W. Davidson (eds) *Organisation of Memory*. New York: Academic Press.

Tulving, E. (1983) *Elements of Episodic Memory*. Oxford: Oxford University Press.

Van Ijzedoom, M. (1995) Adult attachment representations, parental responsiveness, and infant attachment: a meta-analysis on the predictive validity of the adult attachment interview, *Psychological Bulletin*, 117: 387–403.

Vaugh, B. E. and Bost, K.K. (1999) Attachment and temperament: redundant, independent or interacting influences on interpersonal adaptation and personality development, in J. Cassidy and P.R. Shaver (eds) *Handbook of Attachment: Theory, Research and Clinical Applications*. New York: Guilford Press.

Vygotsky, L.S. (1962) *Thought and Language*, 2nd edn. Cambridge, MA: MIT Press.

Waters, E., Vaughn, B.E., Posada, G. and Kondo-Ikemura, K. (1995) *Caregiving, Cultural, and Cognitive Perspectives on Secure-base Behaviour and Working Models: New Growing Points of Attachment Theory and Research* (Monographs of the Society for Research in Child Development), 60(2–3, Serial No. 244).

Watson, M.W. and Fischer, K.W. (1993) Structural changes in children's understanding of family roles and divorce, in R.R. Cocking and K.A. Renninger (eds) *The Development and Meaning of Psychological Distance*. Hillsdale, HJ: Erlbaum.

Watzlawick, P. (1964) *An Anthology of Human Communication*. Palo Alto, CA: Science and Behaviour Books.

Watzlawick, P., Beavin, J. and Jackson, D. (1967) *Pragmatics of Human Communication*. New York: Norton.

Watzlawick, P., Weakland, J. and Fisch, R. (1974) *Change: Principles of Problem Formation and Problem Resolution*. New York: Norton.

West, M.L. (1997) Reflective capacity and its significance to the attachment concept of the self, *British Journal of Medical Psychology*, 70: 17–25.

White, M. and Epston, D. (1990) *Narrative Means to Therapeutic Ends*. London: Norton.

Wiersma, J. (1988) The press release: symbolic communication in life story interviewing, *Journal of Personality*, 56: 205–38.

Index